AN INSPECTOR CALLS: GCSE ENGLISH LITERATURE STUDY GUIDE

DETAILED, ADVANCED AND IN-DEPTH: FOR ANYONE WHO WANTS TO TARGET THE TOP GRADES!

DARREN COXON

CONTENTS

INTRODUCTION

Welcome!

This book is part of the Learning Engineers series of study guides. Each one aims to fully deconstruct each text as well as getting right inside the dark and mysterious world of the examiner, supporting your study and giving you tips to help you get the best grades possible.

Other books in the series:

AQA GCSE English Language Revision Guide

Macbeth revision guide for GCSE

Essay Peasy: how to write any essay for GCSE

If you like this book I'd be very grateful if you'd give it a review. You can link to the review page here if you're reading the Kindle version.

WHAT THIS GUIDE ISN'T

Come on, admit it - this is not the first study guide you've read on An Inspector Calls...

That's ok, I'm not judging. I've looked at a few in my time and by and large they're pretty similar.

Lots of pictures, lots of colour, and they do the basics well.

However, what I've noticed is how few of them really get under the skin of the texts and give you original, insightful things to say that get you the very top marks.

They also often use annoying babyish fonts and cartoons: I've never understood why as you're likely to be fifteen or sixteen and could probably do without them. Or you're a teacher wanting some new ideas, or a parent wanting to help your child. And you just want to be given some interesting ideas and be made to think.

The Examiner's Head series of books aims to change all that. You see, I think that you deserve to have the same sort of inspiring, lights on experience as when you're working with a brilliant teacher in the classroom.

I know it's not the same, but if you can imagine me working alongside you as you read through the play, making gentle suggestions, perhaps urging you to make a note of this or that, and then encouraging you to put what you've learnt to practice, then you might find you experience that same thrill of really understanding something for the first time.

I've been teaching English for more than 20 years, and have taught, led and managed some of best schools in the world, including exclusive Swiss boarding schools, Ofsted Outstanding state schools in the UK, as well as leading education across Brighton College's international schools. As well as having taught across every age range and every ability level, I've also trained and advised teachers the world over. I hope this gives you comfort that you're in safe hands as we navigate the choppy waters of English literature.

WHY 'LEARNING ENGINEERS'?

Bit of a strange name, isn't it? What has engineering got to do with learning English? Look at it this way: every text you study, whether it's a novel, play, poem or piece of non fiction, has its own set of moving parts. This might be how language is used, the way in which the words are structured, or perhaps punctuation.

A writer's job is a little like an engineer's in that they have to take these parts and mesh them together so they work really well. Cogs and levers on their own are useless, in the same way that all the words in a dictionary don't make a work of genius.

The texts you study have been crafted by those who have really mastered these arts. And it's your job to take these literary engines apart and explain how they work.

So when we talk about engineering we don't mean oil and cogs, or wires and circuitboards. We mean words, sentences, punctuation, and so on.

You'll notice that the approach I take when structuring these guides is to follow the process and learner engineer would take when mastering their craft. We first of all look at the story, play or poem engine, listen to it, try to get a sense of how and why it works. We will then take it apart, piece by piece, and examine each of these parts to understand how it fits into the broader whole. How character fits into setting, or how certain characters might use certain language or be described in a certain way.

Just make sure you have an oily rag handy to wipe your hands down afterwards!

1

THE PLAY

INTRODUCTION

As we begin, remember the approach we will take. We start with a broader overview, to understand the play as a whole, before we start to pull the play apart.

I've often had students say at the start of the course that picking apart texts like this might spoil the joy of reading for pleasure. That too much analysis and deconstruction can ruin a book. I don't agree. I've always thought that the arts are so much more enriching if we take the time to understand what has gone into making them, whether this be a novel, a play, or a painting.

I hope that, as we get deeper into *An Inspector Calls*, you feel this too.

J.B. PRIESTLEY

John Boyton Priestley was born in Bradford, Yorkshire in September 1894. He left school aged 16 and decided not to go to university as all he wanted to do was write. He became a junior clerk at a wool firm whilst writing in his small front attic bedroom.

He joined the infantry at the start of the First World War, and by the time he left the army in 1919 had seen front line action and been close to death on a number of occasions. These experiences had a direct impact on his writing.

After university, Priestley took up a place at Cambridge University to read Modern History and Political Science. However, in spite of successfully completing his degree he decided not to pursue an academic career and instead began work as a freelance writer in London. He achieved considerable success through the 1920s as an essayist, and after writing two well received novels began his career as a playwright.

Priestley established himself as one of the most popular of London playwrights, writing several well received plays, including An Inspector Calls, arguably his most famous play.

Priestley wrote the play in only one week, but because the blackout meant that no theatres could perform it, it was first performed in Moscow, before being performed in London the year after.

As well as continuing to write plays, during the war Priestley wrote weekly reflections broadcast on the BBC. However, these were cancelled as the BBC felt them too critical of the government.

Priestley died in 1984 at the age of eighty-nine.

A LITTLE CONTEXT

An Inspector Calls was written in 1945, but is actually set in 1912.

Why does Priestley set the play at this time? When we come to look more closely at the play's themes we'll understand this more, but for now all we need to know is that the play is set in April of 1912, a few days before the sailing of the Titanic.

This is important because one of the main themes of the play is **the impact of progress on the working class**: many of the characters talk positively about the forward march of progress and care little for its impact on common people.

Of course it's **ironic** that they talk about the Titanic as some shining example of progress only a few days before an iceberg sunk it. More on irony later.

There's a lot of arrogance shown by most of the characters, and Priestley wanted to show how this arrogance could be used against the characters to demonstrate how unpleasant these people are and how fragile their self confidence actually is. That it's just a facade and that under the surface there is little stability.

1912 is also just two years before the First World War. As mentioned above, Priestley fought in this war, and it influenced him greatly.

So what we see is Priestley looking back at a critical moment in history and using it to comment on that time he was writing: just at the end of the second world war. He's writing about the world just before the first terrible war, from the position of someone who has lived through these two wars. It's the gap between when he wrote, and the time the play is set, that gives the play such ironic power.

We'll see this in a lot more detail as we explore the play in more depth.

Going deeper

I'll add these little asides as we go through the play as they can help to add further insight. Think of them as little sparks of originality, short detours where we explore the sorts of ideas that will move you up into the very top grades should that be where you wish to head (and I'm sure it is).

The world of the turn of the century was a time of great change but also great self doubt. The Victorian era of progress, which saw the world change unrecognisably, had given way to the modernist period, which began to examine the nature of who we are and what our purpose was on this earth. Have a look at T.S. Eliot's 'The Wasteland' for a brilliant example of this radical self doubt.

This, coupled with the fact that Priestley wrote the play at the end of the second world war, makes this even more powerful, as he had witnessed first hand the machines first designed through the Victorian era being used to destroy countless millions of innocent people.

An audience bruised and bloodied by war could only look at the Birlings with a high degree of cynicism, thinking 'you really have no idea what's in store for you.'

THE STRUCTURE OF THE PLAY

The play is divided into three acts. That's quite normal for plays like this - most plays will be divided into either three acts or five.

Why? Because humans like structure. We actually have it hardwired into our brains. Stories, whether they are told as a play, novel or film, will generally follow a pattern. Introduction, some sort of incident which sets off the storyline, a series of climaxes ending in a final revelation. That sort of thing. You can apply that to pretty much any of the films or TV shows you watch.

This play is no different. It may have an unusual ending, and be a bit spooky, but in fact it's quite standard in the way it's structured:

- **Act One** introduces us to the characters and the arrival of Inspector Goole, which kicks off the storyline. It ends with the revelation that Gerald has had an affair with Daisy Renton and Sheila's humiliated and angry response
- **Act Two** continues straight on from this, and ends with the further revelation that the boy who got Eva/Daisy pregnant was in fact Eric.
- **Act Three** continues straight on from this, and ends with the phone call from the police to inform them that a girl had indeed just died after drinking disinfectant.

What's interesting about the above is that it's the two characters with the biggest social conscience - Eric and Sheila - who are most impacted by revelations at the end of Acts One and Two. Priestley does this deliberately to leave the audience with the biggest emotional impact as the curtain falls.

Before we look really carefully at the play, let's have a quick summary.

SUMMARY

The play is set in one location throughout: the Birlings' home. The Birlings are celebrating the engagement of their daughter Sheila to Gerald Croft, who is the son of one of Arthur Birling's main competitors.

Arthur Birling hopes that this engagement will be beneficial to his business as well as bringing his daughter happiness (we don't have to be a genius to work out which is more important to the man).

After Gerald presents an engagement ring to Sheila, Arthur Birling gives a speech. In it, he talks about how optimistic he feels about the future. He dismisses concerns about a possible war with Germany and talks about the Titanic as an example of the progress being made in industry.

As an audience of course, we are thinking 'aha, that's what you think mate, but we know what happens next and you are so WRONG'. That's an example of irony, by the way - we know more than the character as we know what is about to happen in history (iceberg - glug glug).

He mentions to Gerald that he is up for a knighthood - this is a very high honour only given by the government to a select few influential people every year.

Eric enters, and Birling explains to the two young men how important it is to be self-reliant, and not expect others to look after them or their future families.

It is at this point that the doorbell rings, and a man calling himself Inspector Goole enters. He tells the party that a woman by the name of Eva Smith has killed herself by drinking strong disinfectant.

He asks Birling whether he knows of anyone by that name, and shows Birling a photograph of her. Both Eric and Gerald try to look at the photograph but Goole does not show them.

Birling confesses that he dismissed Eva Smith from his employment nearly two years before. He tells the inspector that there is no way he could have been responsible for the woman's suicide, but the inspector disagrees, telling Birling that this may have started a chain of events that led to her death.

Birling tells the inspector that he fired her because she was part of a group who went on strike because they wanted higher wages.

Sheila enters, and Goole tells her that, after Eva was fired from Birling's business, she took a job at a shop Sheila regularly visited. However, she was also fired from this job because a customer complained about her.

Sheila becomes agitated and asks to see a photograph of the girl. Like before, the Inspector only shows her the photo (can you see a pattern developing here?). Sheila recognises the girl and it becomes clear that she was the customer who complained about Eva Smith.

It turns out Sheila had complained because she'd tried on a dress that she knew didn't suit her, and she thought Eva Smith had smiled at a work colleague as if to say 'doesn't she look awful'. Sheila had threatened to close her account with the shop unless Eva was fired.

The Inspector then goes on to say that, after she had been fired from the shop, she had changed her name to Daisy Renton. At this, Gerald is shocked. (Yes, you can definitely see the pattern, can't you.)

It turns out that Gerald had been having an affair with Daisy Renton, and broke things off with her when he needed to go away on business. He had supplied her with accommodation during their affair, which she had to leave.

The Inspector then shows the photograph to Mrs Birling, and explains that Eva Smith had gone to Mrs Birling's woman's charity only two weeks before, asking for help. Mrs Birling tells the inspector that she had refused to give the woman help, in part because she called herself Mrs Birling, not Eva or Daisy. It also turns out that Eva was pregnant, but not with Gerald's child.

As you may have already worked out (because I'm sure you've watched enough TV drama on Netflix), the baby is of course Eric's. It turns out that Eric had met her in a bar and had begun a relationship with her.

He'd stolen money from his father's office to give to her, as he felt guilty about her becoming pregnant. When Eva/Daisy discovers that the money was stolen, she refuses any more. It is at this point she goes to Mrs Birling's charity for help.

The Inspector concludes his so-called investigation by telling them they are all guilty of her death, and that there are millions of others just like her who are impacted by the actions of people like the Birlings. He suddenly leaves.

Of course, Birling and family are shocked by what they've just heard. They argue amongst themselves about who is most to blame, and it becomes clear that this has affected some more than others (more on this when we look at characters in more depth).

Then, they begin to wonder whether this man was in fact a police inspector. This is confirmed by Gerald, who arrives back and tells them he's done some digging and found out there is no Inspector Goole on the force. Birling calls up the police station and they confirm they've never heard of the man.

Apart from Sheila and Eric, who don't see how anything has changed (as they were all guilty of what the Inspector uncovered), there is much relief in the room as they realise that it was all a hoax.

They even work out that the photograph shown to each of them may have been of different women. It may have been that there was more than one girl. And if this is the case, it may also be that no one committed suicide.

Gerald confirms that there has been no suicide by calling the hospital: but Sheila reminds them all once more that they still acted in a certain way with this girl or these different girls - it takes nothing away from how they all acted towards her. Birling tells them they should laugh it all off.

Just as he says this, the phone rings. It is the police. They inform Birling that a girl has just died after swallowing disinfectant, and that an inspector is on his way to ask them some questions.

The play ends here, without further explanation but with the audience well able to work out what happens next.

ACT 1

A NOTE BEFORE WE START

Before we get into it, I highly recommend you have an open copy of the play in front of you, and a pencil. As we explore the play together, I'd suggest you underline the words and phrases I mention and jot down notes in the margin. This will help you to compile your revision notes, which we'll get onto at the end of the book.

OK, got all that now? Let's begin.

THE OPENING STAGE DIRECTIONS

The directions at the start of the play are important, not just because they give the director an idea of how the scene should be set. We also learn a lot about the characters even before they speak.

The first sentence of the stage directions is a useful place to start. Notice that Priestley repeats 'fairly' - the house is 'fairly large', but not huge, and Birling is 'fairly prosperous'. This immediately tells us that Birling is a social climber: someone who is on his way up, but is not there yet. He is a man with something to prove, perhaps someone who is not completely secure in his position.

We learn that the furniture in the house is 'solid' and that the 'general effect is substantial and comfortable and old-fashioned but not cozy and homelike'. The house is in many ways a physical manifestation of Arthur Birling, its owner. In other words, its layout and furniture is similar to his personality. He is an old-fashioned man, a little cold and pragmatic.

We also learn that on the walls are 'a few imposing but tasteless pictures and engravings'. Again, this represents the tastes of the middle classes: trying too hard but being rather vulgar and tasteless.

The objective correlative

Playwrights will often use setting and props to give further detail about character, mood and theme. This is a good example. Birling's house is described in this way as it very much represents who he and his wife Sybil are. This is a house designed to show wealth, not to give comfort.

We can actually refer to this as an example of the **objective correlative**: objects which somehow represent the inner world of the Birlings. We often use this term to describe how things like weather can show how a character is feeling, but we can also use it to indicate something about a character's personality.

When the curtain rises, we are presented with a scene of the Birlings and Gerald having just finished eating (we know this because of the state of the table and the fact that they're about to have port, an after dinner drink).

What is interesting here is how they are positioned:

- Arthur Birling is at the head of the table, showing him to be head of the family;
- His wife Sybil at the other, showing them to be quite old-fashioned (it's quite a stereotype to think of the mother and father at each end of the table);
- Eric is on one side of the table, Gerald and Sheila are on

the other. The fact that Eric is seated 'downstage' (nearer the audience) means that he could begin the play with his back to the audience. This might be because he is less important at the opening, as the attention is mainly focused on Gerald and Sheila.

We then get a description of **Arthur Birling**. Priestley says that he is a 'heavy-looking, rather portentous man in his middle fifties… rather provincial in his speech'.

This means that he does not have an upper class accent: he may have a fairly large house and run a business, but we can see from the start that he is a self-made man, whose lower-class accent betrays his roots.

On the other hand, his wife, **Sybil**, is described as Birling's 'social superior'. This means that she comes from a higher class family: we can imagine her having inherited some wealth, which perhaps even helped Birling start his business. We don't know that for sure, but Priestley is giving us a clue here about their relationship.

Sheila, their daughter, is described as being 'rather pleased with life', and her fiance **Gerald** as 'the easy well-bred young-man-about-town.' They should immediately give off the impression of being confident, perhaps even a little arrogant. This will become important when we see each of their bubbles burst, one by one.

Eric, on the other hand, is shown as being 'not quite at ease', as if he is unsure of his place in the family.

They are all celebrating and are 'pleased with themselves': again, it's important for us to see that so that when the Inspector arrives their nice, comfortable world can be shattered.

THE OPENING OF THE PLAY TO BIRLING'S SPEECH

Like any good opening, the play introduces us to the characters and their personalities both quickly and effectively.

Take a look at the very first exchange between **Birling** and **Gerald**. Remember: Birling is trying to climb the social ladder, and he sees the marriage between Sheila and Gerald (the son of the businessman Birling is competing with) as a way of taking one more step up that ladder.

Birling mentions the port (a typical upper-class after dinner drink), and tells Gerald that 'it's exactly the same port your father gets'. Birling is straight away linking the drink to the (we assume) more socially superior position Gerald's father is in. It is as if, by drinking the port, Birling is somehow taking in some of that superiority.

Say one thing more

Take a look back at those last 2 paragraphs and see what I did there. That's exactly what you should aim to do when you write your exam essays. In fact, I'm writing this guide to help you both with the content itself, and with how it should be presented.

When you write an English essay, each paragraph should introduce the part of the text you're focusing on, should bring in some quotes, should say one thing about those quotes, and then say one thing more.

The last sentence of those two paragraphs takes you into the grade 9 territory, as it shows you looking really deeply at the significance of the port. More on that later, but I thought it was worth bringing your attention to it now so you can see it repeated throughout this guide.

Gerald refers to his father as 'the governor', which tells us something about his formal relationship with his father, and then goes on to say that 'I don't pretend to know much about [port]'. He responds in quite a relaxed way to Birling, which tells us two things: first of all, he feels welcome into the family, and also that he does not feel intimidated by Birling. In fact, he'll see himself as socially superior to this older, more experienced man, because of the fact that his parents are upper class - Sir George and Lady Croft.

Social class

There'll be a lot more detail on this later, but it's a good time to introduce this theme of **social class**, as we've already seen it showing its ugly face and the curtain has only just risen.

At the time the play was set, social class meant everything. Being born into a higher class meant privilege and wealth. It didn't matter what sort of person you were (and we can see how unpleasant Gerald is as the play develops), you were born into a class and that was that. You could lose all your money and it wouldnt change your class.

On the other hand, if you were working class and made a lot of money in business, the best you could do was move from working class to middle class. You'd never reach the upper classes. And this is because everyone will know where you came from. It might also be seen in how you speak, and what you say to people.

Birling is a brilliant example of this. Notice as the play develops how often he tries to seem a higher class than he is, and how often he makes himself seem foolish. Priestley is a master at presenting us with a man full of his own self-importance, but also one who knows that this status he gives himself is very fragile indeed.

Houses built on sand and all that....

Notice then how **Sheila** chimes in with 'I should hope not Gerald' when referring to him not knowing much about port. She says this 'gaily, possessively': gay in this context has a different meaning to nowadays - it just meant 'happy'. But mixing these two words is interesting: Sheila is perhaps masking a bit of insecurity with her jolly outward appearance. She doesn't want Gerald turning into her father, even though she knows it's probably inevitable.

What this stage direction also shows is that, even though on the surface this is a celebration, there is some tension in the air, some matters that have yet to be resolved. The characters all bring their own baggage into the scene - their hopes, fears, expectations and so on. And in Sheila's case, there is definitely a sense of insecurity very close to the surface.

We'll look more about the role of women later - but for now, it's safe to say that they don't have much power or status at this time, at least not outside the home. She then refers to her mother as 'mummy': we need to see Sheila as having the outward appearance of a little girl even though she is in her twenties. She has lived a rather sheltered life and is naive. Of course, all this will end when the Inspector arrives.

There is then a telling exchange between Birling and **Sybil**. Birling asks Sybil to 'tell cook from me' that the meal was excellent. Sybil reproachfully says 'you're not supposed to say such things', as if telling him off for commenting on the quality of the food in front of Gerald. That is the voice of the upper classes speaking: remember that Sybil is of higher social status than her husband.

The class system is full of rules, and none more so than at the very top. Meal times are particularly tricky places to navigate (and you'll know this if you've ever been to a really nice restaurant and have felt on edge because you're worried about what other people think of you). It's as if Sybil is still teaching her husband how to act in situations like this.

There is an undercurrent of tension in the following exchange between Gerald and Sheila. We know this through the effective use of stage directions. Even though the tone is friendly, Sheila is clearly unsure why Gerald 'never came near' her 'all last summer'. He tells her he had told her before the reason why: 'I was awfully busy at the works all that time' to which she replies 'Yes, that's what you say'.

Even though their tone of voice is lighthearted, there is a lot of tension here. Sheila seems insecure - she doesn't know where Gerald was that summer, and his response is rather defensive and nervy. This is a good example of foreshadowing - a hint of what is to come later in the play.

Etiquette

The reason Sheila doesn't just come right out with it and demand Gerald tell her where he was last summer is because of **etiquette**. This is the set of rules that governs how you act in any one social situation. The world these people inhabit is tightly bound by etiquette, and this will very much be determined by Sybil, who is part of the upper class world with its narrow set of rules as to how one should and should not behave. Girls like Sheila simply should not question their men. There could be no debate.

What this means is that no one actually says what they really think, as they are scared of breaking etiquette. Birling breaks these rules more than most, but this isn't deliberate - he just doesn't know them as well as others as he's new to this upper-class game.

Mrs Birling's response to Sheila gives us a clear indication of the role of women at the time. She says that 'when you're married you'll realise that men with important work to do sometimes have to spend nearly all their time and energy on their business. You'll have to get used to that, just as I did.' She then follows this up with 'Isn't that so, Arthur?'

Now, we could read this as Mrs Birling simply saying that for men, work is often more important than family. But there is another possible reading of this: Mrs Birling will know that men like Gerald and her husband will have affairs with other women, and her response to her daughter is just one more conventional thing to say in 'polite company' to give an excuse for why the husband is hardly ever around. It's like they're in denial, not wanting to face the truth about the men in their lives.

By asking for husband's agreement at the end, she's asking him to be a part of this charade, where everyone says that the husband is busy at work, when actually he's seeing another woman.

Remember: for those higher grades, look for other readings, ways of thinking about the things characters say in different ways. It's not always obvious.

INTRODUCING ERIC

We are introduced to Eric when he 'suddenly guffaws'. A 'guffaw' is a loud, uncontrolled laugh, in response to something funny someone says or does. Sheila asks him 'severely' 'what's the joke?' to which he replies 'I don't know - I just suddenly felt I had to laugh.'

It is true that Eric is a little drunk: we find out later that he has a drink problem. However, what we will also learn is the reason: Eric is aware of the charade everyone is playing around him. He doesn't fit in to his father's pretentious world, and uses alcohol to numb himself.

We'll see a lot more of Eric later, but for now, by introducing him with this laugh, what Priestley does is show how nervous and out of place Eric feels - the laugh is as much a release of tension as anything. He will have been sitting there feeling more and more on edge and suddenly he had to laugh to release some tension.

Birling now stands and gives his important speech. It's worth spending a little time analysing this, as it gives us a lot of information about the time the play was set, as well as introducing a number of the themes and ideas that are explored once the inspector arrives.

BIRLING'S SPEECHES

Birling then rises and 'Clears his throat'. He begins **his first speech** by referring to Gerald's parents, saying that it's a pity they couldn't be at the celebration but that they sent him 'a very nice cable - couldn't be nicer'. He is desperate for their approval, and grabs hold of even the fact they sent a cable as proof that he moves in their circles. There is something rather sad about this desperate need to be liked by people of higher social standing.

He makes an excuse, to say that he actually prefers the gathering being smaller, to which both Mrs Birling and Gerald agree, but the audience knows that he is disappointed that the Crofts couldn't be there, and sees it as a sign that he's not important enough to them to warrant them coming to this engagement dinner.

Eric's response is interesting here: when Birling says that speech making is easier with a larger crowd, Eric says 'Well, don't do any'. Once again we see Eric cutting through the pretentiousness and pompousness of his father. Eric is saying here: 'if you think you need a big crowd to give a speech, and you don't have one here, what's the point of speaking at all?'

Of course, Eric knows as well as anyone that Birling cares little for how many people are gathered to hear him - what Birling is actually saying is that his audience aren't the ones he wants to impress with his speech. He wanted the Crofts there but they cancelled on him and he's not happy about it.

Birling continues by telling Gerald (to whom this speech is directed, in place of his parents) that this engagement means a lot to him. We know why: he wants to get closer to Sir George Croft, and this marriage will enable him to do that. It's one more step up the social ladder.

He even mentions this in the speech, that the two families have been 'friendly rivals in business for some time now - though Crofts Limited are both older and bigger than Birling and Company.' He looks forward to a time when the two companies are working together for 'lower costs and higher prices'.

This is a very old-fashioned approach. There was a time when marriages were arranged between wealthy and powerful families, to further the interests of both. By the 19th and 20th Centuries this practice had all but died out, but we can still see an example of how Birling realises how this marriage will help him to increase his status and make more money.

What we learn is that Birling is not that interested in his daughter's happiness. What he sees here is an opportunity to improve his own social status. To get closer to Sir George's status, which is his ultimate goal.

After Gerald produces the engagement ring, **Birling gives his second speech**. This is the most heavily ironic speech in the entire play, as pretty well everything he says is entirely contradicted by what actually happens next in history:

> "I want to say this. There's a good deal of silly talk about these days - but - and I speak as a hard-headed business man, who has to take risks and know what he's about - I say, you can ignore all this silly pessimistic talk. When you marry, you'll be marrying at a very good time…and soon it'll be an even better time."

He speaks of progress, of Germany not wanting war and about the unsinkable Titanic. However, we know the Titanic sinks. We know the First World War happens, with huge loss of life. But as far as pompous old Birling is concerned, talk of war all just a lot of 'nonsense', because 'there's too much at stake these days. Everything to lose and nothing to gain by war.'

He's right, but it didn't stop the war from happening. Remember that Priestley wrote the play at the end of the Second World War, one with even more devastating war in terms of loss of life (both military and civilian) than the first.

Having fought in the First World War, and lived through the Second, Priestley must have been deeply scarred by the effect of these wars. It is no wonder that we can almost hear Priestley's disgust for a man like Birling as he gives this speech.

And this is when the next big theme is introduced - progress and its impact on the world. Let's take a moment to consider this in response to what Birling is about to say.

Progress

The 19th Century saw some of the biggest advances in engineering in history. The steam engine, telephone, internal combustion engine, the rifle, even electricity - all were invented or discovered during the century before the play was set.

What this means is that, for many, the beginning of the 20th Century was seen as a time when all these great discoveries could be used to advance the human race and make a lot of people very wealthy in the process.

A good example of this is the Rockefeller family. John D. Rockefeller founded the Rockefeller Oil Company in 1870, a business which made him the wealthiest man in the world. He was only able to achieve this because of the advances in engineering that gave him the opportunity to drill for oil.

It is people like Rockefeller who men like Birling look up to. They see the huge potential that is ready to be unlocked by using these new machines. Ways of making processes quicker and more efficient. Mind you, Rockefeller used a lot of his wealth for good purposes. I'm not sure you could say the same about Birling's intentions.

But (there's always a but, isn't there), for every machine that can create opportunity, there is one that can cause misery and death. Take the rifle, for example. Until its invention, battles had to be fought face to face, with swords and spears. The rifle meant that men could be apart from one another and fight from trenches. Hence, the invention of trench warfare. Chemical advances also meant terrible weapons like mustard gas that could be dropped on the trenches.

Now, I'm not saying that slashing someone to death with a sword is preferable to being shot, but as soon as you invent a machine gun or a plane that can drop bombs, one person can kill an awful lot more people than if he was holding a sword. So the chances of mass killings, and also civilian casualties, rose. Hence misery and death being multiplied.

When you look at it this way, you can see that the speech that Birling now gives is about as ironic as the most ironic thing with extra irony on the top. Still not sure what irony is? Well, think about how any audience would respond when Birling talks about how war will never happen and how amazing progress is. Your first response is to think 'ah, if only you knew what was about to happen, you'd likely change your tune'. That's irony.

When Birling says 'the world's developing so fast it will make war impossible', we hear the voice of an entire generation of men who firmly believed in a utopian society, a machine age in which many of the boring, dangerous or inefficient processes humans had done for years would be replaced by machines.

But this is the ironic thing, as we have seen above: machines can kill as well as create. When Birling gives this speech it doesn't even cross his mind. This shows his ignorance, which to be honest is the ignorance of an entire generation of men who thought that nothing bad could happen from progress because it had all been pretty good to that point.

He even mentions the Titanic, saying that it's 'unsinkable, absolutely unsinkable'. Birling has huge pride in what the world has achieved in recent history, and is quite prepared to exploit this for his own advantage.

But that's how it starts, isn't it. People wanting a bigger slice of the pie. Seeing the Sir Georges of this world with more pie than you, and wanting to take it from them. Birling is no different from any greedy capitalist, and Priestley shows this.

His advice to his children, that 'in the forties' there will be 'peace and prosperity' heaps further irony onto everything he says, because of course the thirties saw the Great Depression and the forties saw the Second World War. Not much peace or prosperity in either.

So, we can read this speech as Priestley commenting on how men like this were the cause of these wars and great poverty, by being blind to the reality of a world that had not yet come to terms with what these machines were actually capable of.

After telling Gerald to one side that he may be up for a knighthood, Birling launches into **his third speech**, this time to Gerald and Eric. In it, he tells them that every man has to look after himself and his family, and 'so long as he does that he won't come to much harm'.

He refers to 'cranks' - who we assume he means those dodgy socialists - and their philosophy that 'everybody has to look after everybody else'. Birling doesn't believe in this, saying that 'man has to mind his own business and look after himself on his own'.

And it at this point that the doorbell rings.

This is not an accident. Priestley times the arrival of the Inspector at precisely the moment where Birling is telling the two young men that the only important thing is looking after yourself and your family, and that it is foolish to look after others.

Oh dear - we are about to see the precise results of that, aren't we? Let's meet our friendly Inspector and see what he has to say about this selfish attitude. Watch out Birlings....

THE ARRIVAL OF THE INSPECTOR

Let's take a moment to look at the initial description of the Inspector:

> The Inspector need not be a big man, but he creates at once an impression of massiveness, solidity, and purposefulness....He speaks carefully, weightedly, and has a disconcerting habit of looking hard at the person he addresses before actually speaking.

We can look a little more closely later at his character, but it's interesting to note his name: Goole sounds like ghoul, or ghost. And yet he is described as solid. It is contradictions like these that lend the play a sense of mystery.

We're never quite sure how to read the Inspector, and by the end of the play we question who he was at all. By giving him this ghostly name it brings an element of the supernatural into the play, which is one of the reasons it's still popular today.

The Inspector gets straight to the point - a woman has been taken to hospital having drunk a bottle of disinfectant that has killed her. What's interesting though is how he adds drama to what he says, which doesn't sound very police-ish. He ends by saying 'burnt her insides out, of course.'

He didn't need to add that - it's obvious that if you drink a bottle of disinfectant your insides might suffer (don't try this at home *please*). So what he is trying to do is get an emotional reaction from Birling and the two young men. We will see this develop as the play progresses: the Inspector's role is as much to bring out the truth as a sort of emotional purge, rather than to coldly and clinically investigate.

As we go on in the play, we'll see that the words the Inspector uses are chosen carefully for effect: and he increases the drama of this as he moves on in his enquiry. He will do this to expose the awful truth behind this family of nice manners and upper-class pretensions. *He will use language as a weapon* to burst the bubble I mentioned earlier.

The only reaction he gets from Birling is impatience: Birling cannot see why he is being bothered by this silly man and his investigation. The Inspector cuts in 'massively', something he will do on several occasions throughout the play.

It's an interesting adverb to use, suggesting that during this investigation he is not the least bit interested or intimidated by Birling's money or status. He's the boss at that moment and Birling needs to recognise this and keep it shut.

In fact, what we'll see with the Inspector is that, the more pompous and arrogant other characters' responses are, the more confrontational he becomes. He is looking for a reaction, for a way through that outer layer of respectability, to the ugliness that lies just beneath the surface. Even nice little Sheila won't be spared this.

QUESTIONING BIRLING

The Inspector then mentions Eva Smith's name, and we can sense a small reaction from Birling, a little chink in the armour if you like. And when he shows Birling the photo, the penny drops and Birling changes his tune a bit.

Of course, the Inspector only shows the photo to Birling. When Gerald and Eric try to take a peek the Inspector blocks them, saying 'One person and one line of enquiry at a time.' It's a very clever technique for Priestley to use, as it makes the audience question why he'd do that.

Whereas much of the opening of the play has placed us in a superior position to the characters (because we know what happens in history after the play), as soon as the Inspector arrives we are as clueless as the characters.

We learn that Eva Smith was employed by Birling, but that she was sacked because she'd been part of a group who organised a strike to protest against low pay. When the Inspector questions why he refused their request for a pay rise, Birling is quite shocked. He's not used to having his decisions challenged.

Living in a bubble

Let's go back to this idea of a bubble for a moment. We all live in one: a world where we hear the same things every day and surround ourselves with people who have similar opinions. Family, friends and so on - we naturally gravitate towards those who don't challenge us too much. It's a pretty basic part of human nature.

Birling's bubble is filled with capitalists like him, who think it's every man for himself, that having an affair is normal, that it's all about making as much money as possible and bad luck to everyone else. So when the Inspector asks this question, a little hole is pricked in his bubble. There'll be a lot more holes to come.

What Birling says in response to this challenge is the essence of a **capitalist philosophy** that Priestley is clearly criticising throughout the play. Now, I'm not necessarily saying that capitalism is wrong. It's not my place to give you my political point of view. So when I talk negatively about capitalism or positively about socialism, it's not necessarily my own perspective. I'm taking the point of view of Priestley.

Birling says that he was paying 'usual rates' to the workers, and if they didn't like it 'they could go and work somewhere else'. Of course, and as Eric says, it's not as easy as that, as there might not be other jobs to go to. 'Quite right,' the Inspector agrees.

Birling sees the people who work for him as expendable, like cogs in a machine that can be replaced. He doesn't recognise their essential humanity, that they are flesh and blood and emotions like him, and that sacking people so coldly could set off a chain of events that could end terribly for someone. Just like Eva Smith.

Now, we can look back at the rise of Communism after the First World War, at Stalin and the prison camps and how terrible people were treated in Soviet Russia, and say that it wasn't capitalism that caused this sort of suffering. And there is a lot of truth in that. But when Priestley was writing, what he could see was how the rise of capitalist selfishness had caused so much pain, so maybe it was worth trying a new way of governing.

As my old grannie used to say, hindsight is a wonderful thing. It's the sort of thing grannies say.

Birling refers to the strike as a 'pitiful affair', and says that 'if you don't come down sharply on some of these people, they'd soon be asking for the earth'. He talks about them as he might talk about naughty children who needed to be made an example of.

As owner of the business, Birling sees himself as the father figure, or patriarch. It is up to him to assert discipline on his 'children', even if this means getting rid of a few when they misbehave. It is a deeply paternalistic, patronising attitude but is very common, even today. Powerful businessmen who have built their businesses from scratch will often see them as a family, and so it makes sense that they might view their employees almost as children.

The Inspector's comment is interesting: he says 'it's better to ask for the earth than take it.' What does he mean by this? He could be referring to the fact that men like Birling are taking everything for themselves and leaving nothing for people like Eva Smith. Or maybe he's referring to the plundering of natural resources. At the time the play was written, it's more likely to be the first one.

Whatever the meaning, it's clear that the Inspector deeply dislikes men like Birling and what they represent. He is there to hold the man's ugliness up and amplify it for his family to see. And so far he's doing a good job.

ERIC BUTTS IN

We hear from Eric next; it's the first time he'd had anything to say for himself. And what we hear is a far more socialist attitude than his father. Perhaps it's idealist, perhaps even naive, but there is some truth in what he says, at least from the point of view of Priestley.

Eric says 'why shouldn't they try for the highest possible wages? We try for the highest possible prices.' This is a good point. What's the difference between Birling putting up prices, and people like Eva Smith demanding a fair wage?

Well, to Birling the difference is obvious. He has the power and status to make these decisions, and his workers do not. As he says to Eric, unless he sorts himself out he will 'never be in a position to let anybody stay or go.'

There we have it - it's all about position. Getting there and staying there. If the Eva Smiths of this world are used and thrown away, that's their problem. They should try harder, like Birling did. Birling, the self-made man.

You can feel Priestley's dislike of men like him building as the play progresses.

INTERROGATING SHEILA

Sheila times her entry perfectly, as we have come to the end of the first sad chapter of Eva Smith's life. When Sheila asks what's going on, Birling says 'Nothing to do with you, Sheila. Run along.' Again, that patronising, patriarchal attitude which suggests that none of this business is anything to do with a nice girl like Sheila.

How wrong he is!

Birling's response to the Inspector asking Sheila to wait is the reaction of a man who feels his control slipping away. He tries to pull rank, to assert his status and his connections, but the Inspector is not the least intimidated.

He tells Sheila what happened to the girl, to which Sheila replies 'Oh, I wish he hadn't told me.' Sheila doesn't want anything to burst her little happy bubble, and the Inspector has done just that. We can see that these people are living in denial, either not wanting or not able to face up to the reality of people like Eva Smith. Her life means nothing to them, so why should they care?

That's why the Inspector is there. To make them care.

The next exchange is interesting and is worth spending a few moments on. When Birling realises that there might be others from his family involved in Eva Smith's death, he changes his tune. 'Well, of course, if I'd known about that earlier, I wouldn't have called you officious and talked about reporting you. You understand that, don't you, Inspector?'

What is Birling doing here? On the surface, it would seem that he has become quite nervous, worried that others in his family might have had a role to play in this girl's death.

When he thinks it's just about him, there is more opportunity to control the narrative and less any impact on him and his reputation. But as soon as he realises that others might be involved he tones down his aggressiveness because he suddenly realises this man could damage him through his family.

But there is another, more cynical reading. He perhaps realises that there are others here who are *more* responsible than him, and he is prepared now to cooperate with the Inspector to lessen his own guilt.

Remember: every man for himself. Even if it involves family.

———

Have a look at how the Inspector describes the next stage of Eva Smith's life. He refers to her as being 'lonely, half-starved', and 'feeling desperate'. Sound like the language of a policeman? Of course not. And this is the whole point. By now the audience is beginning to wonder who this strange man is and how he knows these intimate details of her life.

He goes on to add his own opinion, how 'There are a lot of young women living that sort of existence....If there weren't, the factories and warehouses wouldn't know where to look for cheap labour.' Eva Smith is representative of a whole class of people who are used and thrown away by men like Birling. We call them collateral damage - the unavoidable side effect of progress.

Yes, it's pretty obvious which side of the fence Priestley is on here. And it ain't the side of the capitalists.

We then move onto Sheila's realisation that she was part of the girl's suicide. Eva Smith had been taken on by Milward's, a department store.

By now you might have noticed the Inspector's interrogation technique. He tends to lead the characters on, to make them think that what he is talking about has nothing to do with them, before springing a surprise on them. He tells them about how much Eva

Smith enjoyed working at the shop, how she felt she was 'making a good fresh start' and 'settling down nicely', before telling them that she was fired because someone made a complaint about her.

And, as you might have guessed, that person was Sheila. By not telling them straight away, the characters are made to fill in the gaps, which both adds to audience drama and character discomfort.

Once again the Inspector shows Sheila the photograph and does not let others see it. Sheila 'gives a half-stifled sob, and then runs out.' Birling is angry, and tells the Inspector that his arrival has made a 'nasty mess' of the 'nice family celebration' they were having.

As you might expect, the Inspector is right back at Birling, saying 'That's more or less what I was thinking earlier tonight....A nice promising life there....and a nasty mess somebody's made of it.' Once again, he turns their words against them, turning the mirror on them so they might see their ugliness.

The Inspector makes an interesting observation when Gerald says 'we're respectable citizens and not dangerous criminals'. He responds by saying 'Sometimes there isn't as much difference as you think. Often, if it was left to me, I wouldn't know where to draw the line.'

This is an interesting quote to ponder. When you think about it, he has a point. I mean, apparently even Hitler was nice to his mother. Within one group we may be seen as an upright, model citizen. But in order to maintain this status we may need to trample on those beneath us, not caring what happens to them.

So when we talk about good versus evil, we need to be careful. Everyone has a good and dark side, but it would appear that some people find it easier to treat others badly if it benefits them. It's something to think about.

Gerald then replies to the Inspector in what is a rather arrogant manner: 'Fortunately, it isn't left to you, is it?' What he's saying here is that the Inspector isn't important, so has no ability to decide what is right and wrong. It's men in power like Gerald's father who have more say.

But, on this particular occasion, the Inspector does have some power, and is quite prepared to use it to get a confession from everyone there.

When Sheila returns, she admits that she was angry with Eva Smith because she thought she was being laughed at. Sheila had tried on a dress that she knew didn't suit her and had seen Eva smiling to a work colleague.

Sheila was convinced that Eva was smiling as if to say that Sheila looked awful in the dress. Sheila's pride was wounded and she lashed out, insisting the girl be fired from the job or she would take her money elsewhere.

When you think about it, it's such a petty thing that had such huge consequences, and the Inspector makes everyone realise this. Sheila admits it was her fault, not Eva's, and feels ashamed.

Of all the characters, Sheila is the one who most admits her fault, which maybe tells us something about her generation and their understanding of what capitalism had done to the working classes. More on this when we look at Sheila's character.

What is clear is that we are already starting to see that Eva Smith generated negative emotions in each of the characters - in Birling it was greed, and in Sheila jealousy. Sheila was jealous of this pretty girl with 'soft fine hair and big grey eyes', who had tried the same dress against herself and 'it just suited her'. 'She was the right type for it, just as I was the wrong type,' Sheila says.

She may have only been a lowly shop girl, but Sheila believed that Eva was prettier than her. She even admits that 'if she had been some miserable plain little creature, I don't suppose I'd have done it.' She ruined this girl's life because she was jealous of her. Not a great look, Sheila.

We'll shortly see what emotions were generated in Gerald, Sybil and Eric.

The butterfly effect

Have you heard of this? When a small event can cause a chain of events that ends with a much bigger event. Like a butterfly beating its wings in Japan and a hurricane occuring in New York. That sort of thing.

This part of the play begins to explore this idea of the butterfly effect. On its own, Sheila getting the girl fired didn't cause her suicide, just as Birling firing her was not the only factor. But one thing follows another, and Eva's life soon slips out of control. The Inspector is trying to make them realise that, even if they weren't solely to blame, this butterfly effect ultimately caused her death.

THE ACT ONE CLIMAX

Most of us by now are looking forward to the Inspector getting stuck into Gerald as, well, he's not exactly made himself likeable, has he? He's constantly and arrogantly challenged the Inspector and seems to care little about this girl or what happened to her.

But this all changes when the Inspector mentions that Eva Smith changed her name to Daisy Renton. At this point Gerald suddenly asks for a drink, and, rather than begin the interrogation then and there, the Inspector leaves the room, so that Gerald and Sheila are alone.

Why does he do this? It's pretty clever of him I think. He wants Sheila to put two and two together and come up with 'affair' rather than a four (sorry terrible pun). It's much easier for him to press home an advantage if Sheila already knows about the affair and Gerald is on the back foot. Good tactics.

Gerald begs Sheila to say nothing to the Inspector, to which Sheila laughs 'rather hysterically', saying 'Why - you fool - he knows! Of course he knows.' Sheila has begun to work something out: there is something about this Inspector that is not normal, and that he is in possession of way more information than any of them know.

The curtain falls on a 'crushed' Gerald and an Inspector appearing, 'looking steadily and searchingly at them.'

Now it's time for Gerald to feel the full force of the Inspector.

12 KEY QUESTIONS ON ACT 1

After each section, I'll give you a few questions to support your revision.

- What do we learn about Birling from the opening stage directions, both in terms of how he is described and how his home is described?
- What in the opening exchange between Birling and Gerald suggests to us that both men are trying to impress each other? And why do you think they are doing this?
- What immediately indicates to us that Sybil wishes to control how the family speak and act, and why does she do this?
- What suggests to us that Sheila is quite an immature, naive girl at the start of the play?
- What suggests to us that there is some tension between Gerald and Sheila before the Inspector's arrival?
- Why do you think Eric suddenly 'guffaws' (laughs loudly)? What does this tell us about him?
- What do Birling's speeches tell us about his character and about capitalism in general? Why are these speeches so ironic?

- How does Priestley make the Inspector's entrance dramatic and meaningful?
- What does Birling's attitude towards Eva Smith tell us about how he sees those who work for him? What does this tell us about capitalism?
- Why does Sheila have Eva sacked? What does this tell us about her?
- What sort of picture does the Inspector paint of Eva Smith? Why is this unusual for a police officer? Why does he do it?
- What is the 'butterfly effect' and why is it relevant to this play?

ACT 2

THE OPENING OF ACT TWO

Act Two begins exactly where Act One left off. So why bother to break it at all? It's quite a common technique: if any of you watch shows like *The Walking Dead* (or any of the shows on Netflix or Amazon) they'll nearly always end on a **cliffhanger**.

This is a technique that makes the audience want to watch more: it's like we take in a deep breath and wait to see what happens next, and then we have to wait to see. 24 is the worst for this. The number of times I've said 'just one more', and ended up watching eight in a row. Damn you, 24…

So by ending Act One just before Gerald's interrogation, the audience is nicely expectant and cannot wait to see more.

The Act begins with Gerald trying to remove Sheila from the room, as much as anything because he knows roughly what is to follow. When Sheila tells him she'll stay, he says 'Why should you? It's bound to be unpleasant and disturbing.'

The Inspector asks whether Gerald thinks 'young women ought to be protected against unpleasant things'. Gerald says yes, if possible.

'Well, we know one young woman who wasn't, don't we?' the Inspector says.

Once again, the Inspector is using the characters' words against them, to draw attention to their hypocrisy. Sheila should be protected from unpleasantness as she is of a higher class than Eva/Daisy, who did not deserve the same care. That's what Gerald is implying and what the Inspector exposes.

Slowly but surely, the truth that sits behind the surface appearance of the characters is being exposed. Gerald believes that Sheila only wants to stay because 'you've been through it and now you want to see someone else go through it.' Gerald shows that he cares little for Sheila's emotions, believing that her motives are purely selfish.

But the Inspector understands why Sheila wants to stay. He can see that she feels responsible, 'And if she leaves now, and doesn't hear any more, then she'll feel she's entirely to blame, she'll be alone with her responsibility'.

Sheila agrees, saying 'I know I'm to blame - and I'm desperately sorry - but I can't believe - I won't believe - it's simply my fault...' Notice how the speech is broken up with dashes: this is to show the actor playing Sheila that she should speak in short, breathless sentences, emphasising her hysteria.

The response from the Inspector is one of the most important in the play. He says 'You see, we have to share something. If there's nothing else, we'll have to share our guilt.'

Let's consider for a moment why this is so important. The play revolves around one event, the apparent suicide of a young girl caused by a series of events in which each one of the Birling family and Gerald were involved. The Inspector's role is to make them understand that there is guilt that has to be shared.

Sheila understands this straight away: it may be that the world is unequal, that families like the Birlings and Crofts do not believe in sharing. But when something terrible happens, the one thing that can unite us is our sense of responsibility and our guilt. And if we

44

don't have that then who, or what, are we? What have we become?

It's a sobering thought which Priestley explores effectively in this part of the play.

THE ARRIVAL OF MRS BIRLING

When Mrs Birling arrives, Sheila has already worked out that the Inspector's role is to break open each of the characters and let all the bad stuff out. He does this by giving them opportunity to speak and then turning their words against them.

So when Mrs Birling begins by saying 'I'm Mrs Birling, y'know…I don't think we can help you much', Sheila immediately tries to warn her: 'We all started like that - so confident, so pleased with ourselves until he began asking us questions.'

Like her husband, Sybil Birling will be a harder nut to crack. But the Inspector has all evening, and doesn't seem the least bothered by her dismissive tone.

It is when Mrs Birling says 'And in any case, I don't suppose for a moment that we can understand why the girl committed suicide. Girls of that class - ', Sheila becomes even more agitated.

It's clear why. Sheila knows that it is this arrogant, upper class, superior attitude that the Inspector hates so much, and that her mother 'mustn't try to build a kind of wall between us and that girl. If you do, then the Inspector will just break it down.'

As we move towards the centre of the play, so the key themes begin to be explored in more depth. Responsibility, cause and effect, appearance and reality: all of them bound up in a class system that seems to give some people the right to treat others like dirt and think they can get away with it.

But not any more. As Mrs Birling speaks, continuing with her snobbish, dismissive attitude towards the Inspector and his investigation, so both Sheila and Gerald urge her to stop.

Why? Because they can see that things like class and social status mean nothing to him. He is only interested in one thing: the truth. In holding this up to them all so they can see how ugly they have been. And the more Mrs Birling shows her ugliness, the worse it will eventually be for her.

Of course, she can't see that at the moment. She is too caught up in her own self-importance, and that her husband 'was Lord Mayor only two years ago.' But she'll soon see, and by then it will be too late.

There's an expression - 'give someone enough rope and they'll hang themselves'. It means give a guilty person enough time to speak, and before long they'll show their guilt. It's even referred to in the play: Birling says 'I don't propose to give you much more rope', to which Sheila replies 'No, he's giving us rope - so that we'll hang ourselves!'

This is precisely what the Inspector is doing. He actually has to say very little; just let them be themselves and before long they show their guilt. As I say above, it's easier for some than others - Sheila 'fesses up quickly. But some of them are harder to break down.

Let's look now at how he deals with our friend Gerald.

INTERROGATING GERALD

The Inspector begins by 'sharply turning on Gerald' and asking 'Mr Croft, when did you first get to know her?' Notice the phrase, deliberately chosen. Not 'when did you first meet her', but 'get to know'. There is a clear implication in this - it wasn't a one off meeting but a process of 'getting to know'.

At first Gerald denies knowing her, but it is pointless as the Inspector 'knew already'. Gerald admits that he met her at the Palace bar where he'd gone for a drink. Sheila's bitterness clearly shows, and at one stage the Inspector has to tell her to 'be quiet'.

Gerald goes on to give some detail about the evening he met her. He says that she had been 'wedged into a corner' by 'Old Joe Meggarty, half-drunk and goggle-eyed'. When Mrs Birling queries

46

whether he means 'Alderman Meggarty', both Gerald and Sheila tell her that he a notorious womaniser and drunk. An Alderman is a member of local government, so someone with considerable status.

It would appear that the world Sybil Birling is part of is not so nice and polite after all. 'Well, we *are* learning something tonight!' she says.

She is about to learn more. Gerald tells them that he talked to Daisy Renton and heard her story, and when he realised she was hungry got her something to eat. 'And then you decided to keep her - as your mistress?' The Inspector asks.

Mrs Birling is shocked at this, which suggests to us that what she said at the start of the play, about men sometimes needing to spend more time at work, is in fact genuine: she is totally naive to what men like Gerald and her husband get up to when they are out of the house.

She is learning a lot tonight. Which is the whole point of the Inspector being there in the first place. As we see later in the play, his role is not really to learn more about why Eva/Daisy killed herself (as he knows that already). He is there to break apart this family's prejudices, snobberies and lack of care for others, and show them for who they really are.

He's doing a pretty good job of it so far, I'd say.

Gerald then explains that he moved Daisy Renton into the rooms of a friend of his, and it was only later that he began to 'make love to her'. He wants to make clear to the Inspector that his intentions were honourable - he wanted to help the girl, not seduce her.

However, it isn't long before he begins an affair with her. 'I suppose it was inevitable,' he says. 'She was young and pretty and warm-hearted - and intensely grateful. I became at once the most impor-tant person in her life'.

This brings us to another theme of the play - **gender roles and expectations**. The fact that Daisy Renton was so dependent on Gerald made him feel powerful and in control, and these are strong emotions for any man. To have a young, pretty woman so devoted to him was always going to be attractive to a man like Gerald.

We get the sense that Sheila isn't like Daisy. She seems a bit, well, high maintenance, don't you think? A bit of a daddy's girl, spoilt and demanding. That's not to say that she doesn't go through a big change in the play and grow up a lot - more than any other character in fact. It's just that, before all this, my guess is she was quite hard work.

So when Daisy came along, all needy and pretty, seeing Gerald as her 'Fairy Prince', he's bound to be attracted to her. At least that's the reason he's giving. As if he had no choice in the matter.

Of course, on the other hand we can argue that he was taking advantage of a woman in need, and that he was only sorting her out with somewhere to live so he could then have an affair with her. How honest is he being with himself? Probably not very.

At least when he admits that 'any man' would have done the same, Sheila can see that there is some honesty there. 'That's probably about the best thing you've said all night,' she tells him.

The tragedy of Eva/Daisy's life becomes clear when Gerald breaks off the relationship. He has to go away on business for a few weeks 'and by that time Daisy knew it was coming to an end'.

He says that she took it well, that she was 'very gallant' about it. He found this difficult because 'she knew it couldn't last - hadn't expected it to last'. Eva/Daisy had been so beaten down by life, by the things that had happened to her, that she believed that she didn't deserve to be happy, at least not for long. She knew that something that good would not last.

For Gerald, he could see that he had let her down, and wanted to be blamed for this. But her lack of blame made the imbalance between the two of them even more obvious. She simply did not deserve someone like him, at least not for long.

After his interrogation, Sheila gives Gerald back the engagement ring. She tells him that 'I don't dislike you as I did half an hour ago' and that 'You and I aren't the same people who sat down to dinner here. We'd have to start all over again, getting to know each other -'

It is interesting to note that the Inspector seems to have achieved what he set out to do, at least with Sheila and Gerald. Sheila recognises that something has broken between them, but that it needed to happen in order for something potentially stronger to grow in its place. The Inspector has torn down the superficiality of their relationship and laid bare how it was built on sand. Perhaps with a firmer foundation they may now have a chance.

For the first time in the play, Birling attempts to interrupt and disagree, but Sheila tells him not to interfere. Birling does not respond. There has been a shift in power in the house, a new recognition that Sheila is no longer a little girl, and has found her voice. She no longer needs her father to answer for her. It's quite a transformation!

She seems a much better person now, don't you think? Well done, Inspector. But can he work his magic on the others? That remains to be seen.

Time to question Mrs Birling

After Gerald leaves, the Inspector shows Mrs Birling the photograph. When she tells him dismissively that she does not recognise the girl, the Inspector says 'You're not telling me the truth.' Now, this is pretty direct from a man who Sybil Birling would consider an inferior.

Remember: she's all about social standing, hierarchy, where you are on the pecking order. People like *him* simply DO NOT speak to people like *her* in that way! You can imagine her brain trying to work out what to do and say next.

Instead, Birling butts in and says 'you'll apoligise at once', again as if talking to a child. Of course, the Inspector is right back at him saying 'for what, doing my duty?' Good answer.

You'll notice that the Inspector always knows exactly what to say to get the desired response from each member of the family. The more pompous and indignant the response, the cooler and more professional he becomes.

It won't last - he will start to get angry, but again this is all to achieve a certain effect. He is utterly in control throughout. You have to respect him for that.

When Birling mentions that he is a 'public man', which brings with it a certain expectation of respect from others, the Inspector mentions that public men 'have their responsibilities as well as their privileges.'

You won't be surprised to hear that this is pretty important: as I mentioned earlier, this central section of the play is when some of the bigger issues start to be explored in more depth.

What does the Inspector mean? Men like Birling rise to important, influential positions, and with those positions comes a certain level of privilege. This might be money, how people look up to you, how easily it is do progress your business and so on.

But along with this level of privilege comes a degree of responsibility. To ensure those who work for him are treated well. Not to act unethically. Not to bully or intimidate. To listen as much as to speak.

In other words, all the things that Birling is guilty of *not* doing. Birling is a bully. He's selfish and greedy. He never listens and loves the sound of his own voice. He is all privilege and no responsibility.

Of course, Sheila can spot exactly what the Inspector is saying here. When Birling says 'you weren't asked to come here to talk to me about my responsibilities,' Sheila says 'I'm beginning to wonder.'

Sheila understands more and more clearly that the Inspector's role is not as the others believe it to be. As the play moves on, she's the only one who is starting to question his motivations, and even who he is.

She tells her parents that 'we've no excuse now for putting on airs': in other words, they need to stop making themselves out to be somehow better or more important than people like the Inspector and Eva/Daisy. Because the more they do that, the harder they will eventually fall.

The Inspector's interrogation of Mrs Birling is shorter than the others. This may be because her interaction with Eva Smith is quicker than with, say, Gerald. Eva comes to her charity to ask for help, and Mrs Birling refuses.

She gives a number of reasons why. Eva used Mrs Birling's name, her story seemed false, she seemed to not be a good case for assistance. What is telling here is that Mrs Birling does not seem sorry for what she did. 'I did nothing I'm ashamed of or that won't bear investigation', she says.

Now, as an audience we're thinking 'nooooo, Mrs Birling, stop right there! Were you not listening to your daughter? You're digging yourself a big hole!' But of course this is why the play makes for such good drama. As we are now waiting to see how the Inspector bursts Mrs Birling's supersize bubble.

He does it by mentioning two things. First of all, that Eva/Daisy was pregnant. As you can imagine, Sheila is horrified with this, but Mrs Birling simply says 'I'll tell you what I told her. Go and look for the father of the child. It's his responsibility.'

The Inspector presses forward, using emotive language to try to get some sort of reaction from Mrs Birling: 'She was here, alone, friendless, almost penniless, desperate. She needed not only money, but advice, sympathy, friendliness…And you slammed the door in her face.'

Mrs Birling continues in the same manner, impressing on the Inspector that it was the father of the child's responsibility to look after her. But what she says next really gets to the heart of the matter, and the reason why Mrs Birling simply did not believe this girl.

When Mrs Birling asks Eva/Daisy why the father of the child was unable to help, the girl gives a response which, in Mrs Birling's opinion, was 'a lot of silly nonsense'. When asked to say more, Mrs

Birling says that 'she was claiming elaborate fine feelings and scruples that were simply absurd in a girl in her position.'

The dehumanisation of the lower classes

Let's take a moment or two to dig into this and see what we uncover (you may have noticed I like doing this, and it's exactly what you need to do when you write about the play).

Mrs Birling is saying that lower class women like Eva Smith cannot have the sorts of refined feelings of women from Mrs Birling's class. It is as if Eva is somehow less human, less developed than the Mrs Birlings and Sheilas of this world.

We can look at this in the context of much that happened in the world leading up to Priestley writing the play in 1945. Think about how the Nazis dehumanised the Jews, referred to them as somehow being subhuman.

If enough people in power say it, then the population will start to believe it. This is what happened throughout the 1930s in Germany, so that by the time the Nazis came to set up concentration camps, many of those involved firmly believed that Jews were vermin in need of extermination. Not human at all.

It's not quite so extreme here, but you can see how things like the concentration campus, or the genocide in places like Rwanda, starts with people like the Birlings thinking that women like Eva are not capable of the sorts of human emotions they may experience themselves.

(By the way, don't be afraid to bring in contextual ideas when you write, just like I'm doing here. It's one way of showing original thinking which can get you the higher grades. Just remember not to go too off track: the odd sentence or two here and there can really freshen up an essay.)

I think the Inspector gives a first class response here - as we have come to expect: 'Her position now is that she lies with a burnt-out inside on a slab.' Note the brutal, cold language he uses here, in direct contrast to the more refined language Mrs Birling uses. All deliberate, using language as a weapon.

We can see that the Inspector is losing patience with these people. When Birling once again objects, he says 'Don't stammer and yammer at me again, man.' At this, Birling sits. Birling seems beaten, and by sitting down shows that the Inspector is in a more superior position at this stage.

Over the next few minutes, the Inspector questions Mrs Birling, constantly leading her where he wants her to go. It is only when he makes her admit that the man who got Eva Smith pregnant is 'the chief culprit' and 'ought to be dealt with very severely' that Sheila (of course) realises where this is heading. Not sure why it took her so long…

He has led Mrs Birling to say exactly what he wanted her to say. That the Inspector has a duty to make sure the man is 'compelled to confess in public his responsibility.' That it is the Inspector's 'duty' to ensure this is done.

Of course, when he does not move, Mrs Birling questions this, to which he replies that he is waiting to do his 'duty'. And then the penny drops….

As we reach the climax to Act 2, Mrs Birling suddenly realises where all this has been leading. Her stuttering response, shown through Priestley's use of elipses (dots between phrases), is a powerful way to illustrate how this woman's world has just come crashing down around her.

As in Act 1, it is Sheila who has the last word. 'I begged you and begged you to stop', she says, before the door opens and Eric appears, 'looking extremcly pale and distressed'.

Things are teed up nicely for the final act's twists and turns. And oh boy, are there a few of those.

12 KEY QUESTIONS ON ACT 2

- Why does Priestley bother to split the scene between Sheila and Gerald, continuing Act 2 exactly where Act 1 left off?
- Based on what he tells Sheila at the start of Act 2, what does the Inspector want the family to share? Why is this important to him?
- Why does Mrs Birling act in the way she does with the Inspector? What does this tell us about her?
- What does Sheila mean when she says 'he's giving us rope - so that we'll hang ourselves!'?
- What does the way in which Gerald treats Daisy Renton tell us about his character in relation to women?
- In what ways does Daisy seem different to Sheila?
- Why does Sheila say 'I don't dislike you as I did half an hour ago'? Why has her attitude towards Gerald changed, and what does this tell us about how Sheila herself is changing?
- What does the Inspector mean when he says that public men like Birling 'have their responsibilities as well as their privileges'?
- Why does Mrs Birling continue on in the way she does with

the Inspector even when Sheila is desperately trying to make her stop?

- What is significant about Mrs Birling saying about Eva/Daisy: 'she was claiming elaborate fine feelings and scruples that were simply absurd in a girl in her position'?
- What shows us that the Birling no longer has any control of events, and that the Inspector is fully in charge?
- Why does the Inspector allow Mrs Birling to hold the 'father of the child' entirely responsible for Eva's final condition before revealing who that young man is?

ACT 3

THE INSPECTOR CONCLUDES AND LEAVES

As in the break between Acts 1 and 2, Act 3 begins exactly where Act 2 left off.

Unlike the others, Eric begins by acknowledging the fact that the Inspector knows everything already. Like Sheila, he realises that hiding things from this man will only make matters worse. The Inspector will accept nothing but total honesty.

Of course, what Eric doesn't realise is how hard his mother has just made it for him, by 'blaming everything on the young man who got this girl into trouble, and saying he shouldn't escape and should be made an example of'. It reminds us of how her arrogant belief that none of this is her business blinded her from the truth.

When Eric realises that Sheila had told their parents of his drinking habit, he calls her a 'little sneak', in itself rather a childish response. Sheila is calm and mature, telling him that he is being unfair, and that 'I only told her tonight because I knew everything was coming out'.

Sheila can see how there can be nothing hidden any more, and it was better for their mother to know in advance, than during the Inspector's questioning.

True to form, Birling resorts to type, questioning his daughter's 'sense of loyalty'. This is ironic, based on the fact that Birling seemed quite relieved earlier in the evening that he was not solely to blame for the girl's suicide.

The details that Eric then reveals are sordid and unpleasant, and show how low Eva Smith had sunk. Eric had got her drunk (largely because she'd had little to eat that day), went back to her lodgings, insisted on going in with her even though she didn't want him to, and then slept with her.

What is even more unpleasant (if we are to believe Eric) is that he was so drunk that he cannot remember all the details.

From here, Eric begins a relationship of sorts with her. However, we cannot help but think that it's rather a seedy sort of relationship, which ends with Eva pregnant and Eric stealing money to help her out.

Eva descended from her position as respected worker, able to gather support for a strike in protest at poor pay, to a drunken, pregnant woman living in lodgings and seduced by an immature, impulsive young man with an alcohol problem. It's a tragic fall, and has been entirely caused by the people assembled before the Inspector that evening.

On their own, each action did not lead to Eva's death. In combination, it would appear that this respected, wealthy and influential family all but murdered her themselves.

As the questioning continues, so the family begins to finally break apart. Eric finds out that his mother had refused Eva support. 'Then - you killed her!...and the child she'd have had, too - my child - your own grandchild - you killed them both - damn you, damn you - '

This is the climax of the drama, the point at which everything finally comes out. All the buried anger and fear and frustration that the family had been storing up for years and years. The Inspector has opened them up, exposed their ugliness and their dirty, dark secrets. It is powerful stuff.

Just as the scene is about to break into violence, with Eric 'almost threatening' his mother and Birling 'crossing to them', the Inspector interposes. 'Taking charge, masterfully' he shouts 'Stop!'

They all suddenly sit, as if under his spell. He then calmly sums up everything he has learnt. 'This girl killed herself…And each of you helped to kill her. Remember that. Never forget it.'

It is Birling that the Inspector seems to have the most disgust for. 'You started it,' he says to Birling. 'You made her pay a heavy price. And now she'll make you pay a heavier price still'.

As you might expect from the capitalist Birling, he uses money to show his deep regret for what happened. 'I'd give thousands - yes, thousands.' 'You're offering money at the wrong time,' the Inspector replies. A case of too little, too late.

The Inspector's concluding comments are amongst the most profound, and sum up people like Priestley's deep criticism of the rising middle and upper classes with their lack of interest and empathy for those beneath them:

'There are millions and millions of Eva Smiths and John Smiths still left with us, their lives, their hopes and fears, their suffering and chance of happiness, all intertwined with our lives, with what we think and say and do. We don't live alone. We are members of one body. We are responsible for each other. And I tell you that the time will soon come when if men will not learn that lesson, then they will be taught it in fire and blood and anguish.'

Wow. That's quite a final speech! Not exactly the sort of thing you'd expect a police inspector to say, but it certainly hits the mark.

His words are, of course, deeply prophetic: they look to the future, to two world wars and the horrors of the concentration camps. It is as if the Inspector has travelled back in time to the days before everything began to unravel, when men like Birling thought the world was theirs for the taking.

And then the Titanic sank, and millions lost their lives in the filthy trenches of the Somme and Ypres, and even more suffered agonising deaths in the gas chambers or buried alive in their own homes during the Blitz.

In fact, we could almost read it as if the Inspector is Priestley himself, gone back to hold the mirror up to the very people who were part of the problem. To expose them for what they really are.

Remember: this play is not supposed to be read, or watched, as a piece of complete realism. It can be interpreted in a number of different ways precisely because the Inspector himself is shrouded in mystery.

Let's see how the family react to him leaving.

THE AFTERMATH

It would appear that good old Birling has learnt precisely nothing. As soon as the Inspector leaves, the first thing he says to Eric is 'You're the one I blame for this'.

What a great father he is.

Birling continues to rub salt in by saying that 'There'll be a public scandal'. The only thing he's interested in is his name and how others in society see him. This is furthered when he says 'I was almost certain for a knighthood in the next honours' list - '.

Unsurprisingly, Eric reacts hysterically to this, laughing at his father and saying 'What does it matter now whether they give you a knighthood or not?' Mrs Birling chips in saying that she's ashamed of him, to which he replies 'don't forget I'm ashamed of you as well'.

Birling responds in an interesting way to this. He says 'There's every excuse for what both your mother and I did - it turned out unfortunately, that's all.'

Birling believes that he had a reason for firing Eva, just as Mrs Birling had a reason for refusing to help her. And the reason is? Eva challenged them: she challenged Birling's decision to pay her rubbish wages, and challenged Mrs Birling by not being the weak, pathetic creature Sybil Birling expected to see come and ask for help.

So as far as they are concerned, they were in the right. Because, even after everything the Inspector has put them through, they still believe in their own superiority and self righteousness.

Of course, Sheila is the one person who challenges this. 'But now you're beginning all over again to pretend that nothing much has happened...you don't seem to have learnt anything.'

The mood of the play shifts when Eric mentions the moment that the Inspector showed up, just when Birling told Eric and Gerald that 'a man has to make his own way, and that we weren't to take any notice of these cranks who tell us that everybody has to look after everybody else, as if we were all mixed up together...and then one of those cranks walked in.'

Sheila picks up on this, 'Sharply attentive', and questions whether that was 'when the Inspector came, just after Father had said that.' She follows this by querying whether he was 'really a police inspector.'

Sheila then gets to the heart of the matter, when Birling says that it would matter a lot if the man had not been an inspector. 'But don't you see, if all that's come out tonight is true, then it doesn't much matter who it was who made us confess...That's what's important.'

Sheila has a good point. Each of the family confessed to treating Eva/Daisy badly. There can be no denying it. So why does it make any difference whether he was an inspector or not?

Because (as you well know), to the likes of Birling, it's not about how true something is, but rather *how others in society see it*. If he was not an inspector, then the scandal may not get out, and Birling can breathe again.

That's all he's interested in. Not how true it was. But how much it could damage his precious reputation.

Sheila goes on to say that 'all he really did was make us confess. We hardly ever told him anything he didn't know.'

Birling now looks to blame his children for allowing themselves 'to be bluffed'. As far as he's concerned, this man, 'Probably a socialist or some sort of crank...let him bluff you into talking about your private affairs.'

Birling is putting an interesting spin onto things, don't you think? It's what politicians do all the time, hiding behind clever arguments and not facing the truth. It's easy to tell someone what they should have done after the fact, but as Eric says, 'I didn't notice you standing up to him'.

Birling is a weak man, a coward who cannot take responsibility for what happened. He will even throw his own children under the bus in order to come out unscathed.

GERALD REAPPEARS

Birling's weakness is further shown when Gerald reenters. Sheila is happy to tell him everything, but her father replies 'Now-now - we needn't bother him with all that stuff.' Birling is still more interested in preserving his reputation in the eyes of his main competitor's son than he is in the truth.

Gerald then drops his bombshell, telling them that 'That man wasn't a police officer.' The stage directions ascribed to Birling at this point show us how he is feeling: 'excitedly' is used three times. Birling clearly feels that the whole thing has been a hoax, and that he is now off the hook.

Mrs Birling joins in the premature celebrations, saying 'Triumphantly' 'Didn't I tell you?' Birling confirms this with a phone call to the Chief Constable: sure enough, there is no inspector Goole on the force.

It is Birling's comment, and Sheila's response, that gets to the heart of the entire play. When Birling says 'This makes a difference.... it makes all the difference', Sheila responds 'I suppose we're all nice people now!'

Let's take a moment to unpick this in some detail, as Priestley is making a clear comment on all the play's major themes here. As far as Birling, his wife and Gerald are concerned, the fact that the Inspector was not who he says he was means that they are now no longer accused of this young girl's death.

But what Sheila is arguing is that it takes nothing away from how they acted towards Eva/Daisy. Whether she was one person or several does not matter: the fact is, each of them owned up to treating this woman badly. Abusing their position in society to treat a young, vulnerable woman badly.

Birling sacked her because she stood up to him and demanded fair pay, Sheila had her fired from her job at the shop because of Sheila's own insecurities, Gerald and Eric took advantage of her sexually, and Mrs Birling refused her charity because she didn't fit the mould of a helpless girl.

What this fake Inspector has done is used this girl to hold the mirror up to these people and to try and make them see who they really are. How much they take others for granted and believe there can be no repercussions for their actions. How utterly selfish they are, and removed from reality.

Priestley, looking back over two world wars, has the benefit of hindsight: he knows how it was the self-centred actions of those in power, desperate to cling on to their positions at all costs, that sent so many millions of people to their deaths.

Whether it be a young woman or the Jews in the concentration camps, it is still the same belief that those in power are somehow separate from those who are oppressed. That those with wealth are somehow more valuable, and those without can be used and thrown away.

We can now see how this debate is explored between the characters.

The first thing to look at is how each character reacts to the news. Birling and his wife are sensible, pragmatic, and cold: they want to think about how best to respond. As Birling says, 'Now it's our turn.' He seems to be suggested an act of revenge, retaliation. His thoughts immediately turn to how he can be compensated for this hoax. He has already forgotten about the girl.

On the other hand, Sheila and Eric are more emotional. 'Whoever that chap was,' Eric says, 'the fact remains that I did what I did. And Mother did what she did. And the rest of you did what you did to her. It's still the same rotten story whether it's been told to a police inspector or to somebody else'.

Eric wants to look at the facts as they stand: he is more interested in what they did than who uncovered it. However, for Birling, it is always about people and their status. He is exasperated that his children can't see 'the difference between a lot of of stuff like this coming out in private, and a downright public scandal.'

To Birling, it is more about who knows these sordid details than the details themselves. Provided he can keep this contained within his family he can see a way out. But for Eric and Sheila, it is far more about what they did. They don't care who knows.

Their argument is broken by Gerald, who has remained quiet throughout this initial exchange. When Eric says 'it doesn't alter the fact that we all helped to kill her,' Gerald replies asking 'is it a fact?'

He then goes on to pick apart whether a girl died at all. He uses a rational, sensible argument, in many ways more like a traditional inspector. They all admitted 'something to do with a girl', but how do they know 'it's the same girl'?

Gerald reminds them that the Inspector wouldn't show the photograph to everyone, just one person at a time, so it could have been a different photograph: 'We've no proof it was the same photograph and therefore no proof it was the same girl.' He turns to each member of the family, intelligently pulling apart the Inspector's approach, so that by the end we too believe that this may all have been made up.

The final proof of the hoax is Gerald's call to the hospital, who confirm that no girl has died there that evening. Whilst the relief in the house is palpable, Sheila is still insistent on the fact that they did still admit to treating a girl badly. As she rightly says, 'Evrything we said happened really had happened. It it didn't end tragically, then that's lucky for us. But it might have done.'

Sheila says she is 'frightened' how they talk about this, how that now it will no longer damage their reputation they are no longer concerned about what they did. She is frightened because, perhaps for the first time, she is seeing her family for who they truly are: people who care only about themselves and their position in society. How the world sees them is far more important than how weaker individuals are treated.

It is interesting that it's Sheila and Eric, the two youngest members of the family, who are the ones who see the truth. In many ways they show a wisdom their parents sadly lack. Gerald is far more of the opinion of Birling and his wife: he is an ambitious young man who is prepared to side with whoever will further his career.

Once again, Sheila gives us the central message of the play when she says 'So there's nothing to be sorry for, nothing to learn. We can all go on behaving just as we did.' This is not spoken as a question: she realises that the events of that evening will have no bearing on how any of them behave moving forwards. This is profoundly depressing for her.

However (and this is where the final moments of the play still hold their power), it is the impact of the Birlings' inability, or disinterest, in learning from their mistakes, that Priestley wishes to hammer home. Because if we do not learn from our mistakes the world will continue to present us with situations that encourage us to do just that.

This is an interesting way of looking at the world. Some people believe that events in the world just happen randomly, that there is no logic or guiding hand that pushes us in a certain direction. The world is chaotic and uncertain and we have to make the best we can of it. Every man for himself, as Birling advises the two young men at the start of the play.

Others believe that there is a design to the world, that things happen for a reason and that we are presented with situations that help us to move on in our lives, to learn and to grow and to become better people. And that our responses to these events shape the lives of others. We do not live in a vaccum: everything we say and do can have a huge impact on those around us.

Now, one argument that could be levelled at the play is that, because Birling and his wife flatly refuse to learn from the Inspector's visit and interrogation, and are prepared to go on as if nothing had happened, they will be presented with another incident to force them to learn the hard way.

And of course this is exactly what happens. Birling's mocking comment to his children, that they are 'the famous younger generation who know it all' is interrupted by a phone call. And guess what! Yes, you guessed right: it is a call from the police. A girl has just died after swallowing some disinfectant, and an inspector is on his way to ask them some questions.

The curtain falls on them standing 'guilty and dumfounded', and Sheila 'facing the door'. What a great ending! Not many people, when they first watch the play, see that coming. On the surface it may seem a bit of a gimmicky ending, a clever way to shock and audience, a 'twist in the tale' which have always been so popular.

However, if we look at it in the light of what I've just mentioned above, we can see what a powerful comment Priestley is making here. On the personal level it is about how individuals have to learn from their mistakes, or life will keep trying to teach them lessons.

On the political level, there is a clear comment being made about the two world wars: we failed to learn from the First, and so the Second came along to teach us an even bloodier, more brutal lesson. You can sum up Priestley's message in one line:

People - do you never learn?

Let's turn our attention in the next section to each of the characters. This will help us to gain a better understanding how how Priestley uses them as vehicles through which those key themes and ideas are explored.

Vehicles you say? What do you mean?

Read on, my friend, and all will be revealed.

12 KEY QUESTIONS ON ACT 3

- What shows us Eric's immaturity at the start of Act 3?
- What in your opinion makes how Eric treated Eva/Daisy sordid and unpleasant?
- Why is it significant that Eric's confession is last, even though it was Mrs Birling who last saw Eva/Daisy?
- What shows us that the Birling family have finally broken apart?
- What does the Inspector mean when he says 'You made her pay a heavy price. And now she'll make you pay a heavier price still'?
- What is significant about the Inspector's final comments before he leaves the family? What message is Priestley trying to get across, and why do you think he is trying to do this?
- What is the only thing that Birling seems worried about once the Inspector leaves?
- Why does Birling say 'There's every excuse for what both your mother and I did'? What does this tell us about them and why do they differ from Sheila and Eric?
- Why is it unimportant to Sheila whether Goole was a real inspector or not?

- What does each character's reaction to the news the Inspector was a fake tell us about them?
- Why is Sheila 'frightened' at how they are all talking now they have made that discovery?
- Why do you think Priestley ends the play in the way he does, with another phone call and another Inspector on the way? What comment do you think he is trying to make on responsibility?

2

THE CHARACTERS

WHAT ARE CHARACTERS?

If I was to begin this section by saying that the first thing you need to know about fictional characters is that **they aren't real people**, you'd probably say 'well of course not, even I know that.'

But what you might not have thought about before is what the **purpose** or **function** of different characters is in any fictional narrative.

You see, each character in a novel, play, film or TV show has a purpose. And that purpose is to **move the story onwards**. If a character doesn't do that, he or she has no right to be in that story.

They do this by **creating conflict**, as this is the most important tool a writer has at their disposal. It is only when characters are in conflict with themselves and with those around them that we have a storyline.

By conflict, I don't necessarily mean characters fighting with each other (although we get a fair bit of that in this play). I mean characters who come from different backgrounds, have different opinions, and who want different things. If every character in this play agreed with each other it would be pretty boring.

No, the reason this play works is because there is so much internal conflict. All of the characters respond differently to the Inspector, and this causes tension.

So, let's look at how these characters differ, and how Priestley sets up this contrasts in order to explore the main themes of the play.

ARTHUR BIRLING

Arthur Birling is the **patriarch**, the head of the family. And he knows it. He is a man for whom status means everything: it is even more important than his family.

Put simply, **status** is your position in society: how others see you, the amount of power and control you have over others. It is largely down to how much money you have, and how many influential friends.

The reason Birling is so obsessed with getting a knighthood (which would change his title to Sir Arthur Birling) is because it will link him in with important people in the government and therefore give him more status.

He looks up to Gerald's father Sir George Croft because Croft is further up in society than Birling. Croft is more successful in business and has the knighthood: this will hurt Birling, who believes he deserves the same.

Birling's main fault is his **pride**: in drama, we call this level of pride **hubris**: it is an excessive pride that will ultimately destroy Birling, as it blinds him from the truth. He believes he is always right and is not interested in others' opinions unless they confirm his own.

THE OPENING STAGE DIRECTIONS

We get this sense of a purposeful, somewhat bullish man from the opening stage directions. Birling is described as 'heavy-looking' and 'portentous' (which means pompous and overly-solemn so as to impress).

He is someone who puts on an act: he is a man to whom outward appearances are everything. Perhaps a little pretentious, trying too hard to be the serious businessman and important figure in society, but one who cannot hide his roots.

We know this because of his 'provincial speech': this means he speaks with a city accent, not the accent of the upper classes. He might be able to put on an act of being of a higher class, but his accent gives something away. He was not born into money, but married into it. More on Mrs Birling later.

Perhaps we are being overly harsh on Birling. He has clearly achieved some success in business which suggests certain qualities. They might not be overly decent qualities, but nonetheless he has built up his business to the point where he employs a number of staff and lives an affluent life.

However, from the very opening of the play, we see Birling as someone to whom appearances mean everything: both how you look, and how you act. The Inspector will break this apart as the play develops, and we will see Birling for who he really is.

BIRLING IN ACT 1

As Act 1 progresses, we learn a lot about Birling through his interactions with his family and with Gerald Croft. As we explored in the act by act summary, Birling starts by establishing his desire for equal status with Sir George Croft by explaining to Gerald that the port they are drinking 'is exactly the same port your father gets'. Status has a lot to do with the things we associate with class: in this case, port is a **symbol** of wealth - it is an upper class after dinner drink.

However, Birling gives away his background when he tells his wife to thank Cook for dinner. Her response - 'Arthur, you're not supposed to say such things' - tells us that you might be able to surround a man like Birling with the outward appearances of the upper classes, but you cannot fully remove him from his more humble background.

In many ways Birling is a more dangerous animal than the likes of Mrs Birling or Gerald Croft. This is because he feels he has more to prove, which makes him greedier for success and more prone to both aggression and defensiveness. He is terrified of losing everything he has worked for, which explains his response to the Inspector and his relief when Gerald discovers that Goole is fake.

He sees the marriage of Gerald to Sheila in business terms: in many ways this is an almost medieval attitude, like an arranged marriage that would further the business interests of both families. He sees the marriage bringing him closer to Crofts Limited, which in his eyes can only be a good thing.

BIRLING'S FATHERLY ADVICE TO ERIC AND GERALD

Birling's pride shows itself in his belief that he has learned the secret of success, one that he is prepared to share with Eric and Gerald.

In Act 1, after he ironically mentions his belief that there will be no war, he explains to the two young men the importance of looking after yourself and your family. He uses some interesting figurative language when talking about how 'some of these cranks talk and write now': 'you'd think everybody has to look after everybody else, as if we were all mixed up together like bees in a hive'.

Birling does not believe that men like him should look after anyone but himself and his immediate family. He thinks that left-wing writers, by promoting communist thinking, will make everyone think and act the same, 'like bees in a hive'. What Birling is arguing here is that you have to stand out from the crowd and be your own man.

Of course, it is at this precise moment that the Inspector arrives and seeks to tear apart this pretence. Priestley brings the Inspector in at this moment because it is the point at which we see clearly Birling's materialistic, capitalist philosophy; one that men like Priestley believe were the cause of the world wars.

It is the philosophy of many men like Birling (it is even today), so it is important we are presented with it just before Goole arrives, so that we can then understand the effect it can have on those without money and power.

HOW BIRLING RESPONDS TO THE INSPECTOR'S INTERROGATION

We see Birling's utter indifference towards the life of Eva Smith in Act 1, when the Inspector mentions how she died. Birling's impatient response - 'Yes, yes. Horrible business. But I don't understand why you should come here...?' - clearly demonstrates the effect his deeply selfish philosophy has had on his empathy.

The fact is, Birling has none. He cannot put himself in other people's shoes, unless they are the shoes of Sir George Croft, in which case he is desperate to do so.

This attitude continues after the Inspector explains the link between Birling and Eva Smith. Even when Goole tells him that she left his employment, he says that 'it obviously has nothing whatever to do with the wretched girl's suicide. Eh, Inspector?'

Two things are worth noting here. Firstly, the fact that he refers to Eva as 'wretched'. This can mean a number of things, but when used in this context tends to be a term used to express anger and annoyance about a person.

Rather than referring to her a 'poor girl', by using 'wretched' it is almost as if Birling is annoyed that her suicide has interrupted his evening just as it was going so well.

Secondly, by ending with 'Eh, Inspector?', he is trying to use a more familiar approach to get the Inspector on side. We can imagine him using this a lot in his life, to get his own way with those who might be impressed by his status. However, it doesn't work with Goole.

But still Birling holds his original position, saying 'If we are all responsible for everything that happened to everybody we'd had anything to do with, it would be very awkward, wouldn't it?'

OK, he has a point, but I think you can take it too far the other way, which is what Birling does. Of course, we cannot be fully responsible for what happens to others, but equally we shouldn't go through life thinking that nothing we do will impact those around us. It might not happen there and then, but ripple effects occur and small acts can have big consequences later. As I mentioned with the 'butterfly effect' earlier.

When Birling talks about the strike, we again see how he views people like Eva Smith. He calls the strike a 'pitiful affair', as if saying that people like this can't even protest properly. Which may well be the case, if they are hungry and broken.

We sense him seeing them almost like children who need to be disciplined: 'We forgave them…except the four or five ringleaders , who'd started the trouble'. He sounds more like a teacher than an employer.

He refers to them as 'these people', as if they are a different breed entirely from the likes of him. He creates a separation which makes it easier for him to act in a cold and hard way. It is what they deserve, he seems to be saying. They have to be made an example of or 'they will soon be asking for the earth.' Just like misbehaving children.

BIRLING'S ATTITUDE TO SHEILA

On the surface, it would appear that Birling has a fairly traditional view of his daughter. He doesn't want her to get caught up in anything unpleasant, nothing that she should worry herself over. He has tried his best to protect her from the ugliness of life, as much as anything to keep her pure and fresh for her husband to be.

But what this has done is create a somewhat superficial, spoilt child (at least this is the initial impression we have of Sheila). By wrapping her in cotton wool he has ensured she cannot initially cope with the ugly truth of Eva's death.

Birling tries to protect Sheila from the worst of it all, but as the play progresses finds his control of her slipping away. This is inevitable: with every truth that comes out, so Sheila sees her family for who they truly are, which naturally forces a distance between her and them. Her world falls apart, but this is a good thing for her, even if at the time she can't see it.

BIRLING'S CHANGE OF TONE

Notice how, when he realises that it isn't just him involved in this death, he changes his tone with the Inspector. He even apologises, saying 'I wouldn't have called you officious and talked about reporting you' if he had known that others in his family might be involved.

Why does he do this? Is it because of his desire to protect his family at all costs? By now, you probably know the answer. He changes his tune because, if others in his family are involved, the chances of this getting out and damaging his reputation become greater.

Controlling the family

One thing you need to understand about a traditional view of patriarchy (by this I mean a male-controlled society) is that control has to start in the family. The man of the house has to be seen to be in control of his family, with an obedient, loyal wife and well-behaved children, if he is to make a name for himself in society.

The reason for this is simple: the man who can control his family is seen as having the strength and character needed to be successful in life.

This is why so much of history is about how women and children can be controlled. I'm a happily married man, but even I can see how the marriage service, with the father 'giving away' the bride to the husband, is an act of transfer of ownership: from one man to another. Legally, the woman is passive in all this - she has no say in the matter.

Nowadays there are a lot more variations to this tradition, and many couples don't get married for this reason, but the fact remains that the marriage ceremony is one that reinforces a man's control over his wife.

The same can be said of children: that they should obey their father, be seen and not heard, and so on. Even in school, this unquestioning obedience of our elders is one that most simply accept. It does have its place: we should feel we can learn from those who are older than us, and I do think that a certain amount of respect for elders is a good thing, providing those elders offer a good example.

But taken to its extreme it can mean women and children living in fear, and men like Birling doing all they can to maintain control so that the world sees them as a solid family men, and therefore more trustworthy. In the case of the play, it is all a sham: a house built on sand.

Because Birling was directly involved in Eva's dismissal, he can somehow 'control the narrative': in other words, know in advance what is coming up and steer the conversation away from anything that might incriminate him further.

But when it comes to his family's potential involvement? He has no idea what they may have done, so is totally on the back foot. And for a control freak like Birling that is not a good place to be.

His arrogant, bullish attitude with the Inspector may well now back-fire on him, and he is frankly scared of the repercussions. As well he should be.

HOW BIRLING RESPONDS TO THE INTERROGATION OF THE OTHER CHARACTERS

As the play progresses into Act 2, Birling takes more and more of a back seat, challenging the Inspector at times, objecting to his treatment of his daughter, but realising that his control of the situation has disappeared. He is not in charge, and this hurts him.

When he does try to take control, the Inspector raises his game as well. For example, Birling's objection to the questioning of his wife in Act 2 - 'I'm not going to have this, Inspector...I'm a public man' - is met with the Inspector's cutting response: 'Public men...have their responsibilities as well as their privileges'.

As we've explored before, this is a good example of how the Inspector uses the characters' words against them. Like a mirror, remember.

The final put down comes when Birling tries to object to the Inspector's further questioning of Mrs Birling. At the end of Act 2, when the Inspector says 'Don't stammer and yammer at me again, man,' Birling sits. It is this action that shows us that Birling feels beaten. From this point he turns his anger on his family, and not the Inspector. After all, if he can't stop the Inspector from doing his job, perhaps he can have more luck with his family.

HOW BIRLING RESPONDS TO ERIC'S INTERROGATION

Birling saves his most savage criticism for his son in Act 3. We sense from the start of the play that he is disappointed in Eric and sees Gerald as more the son he never had. Both Sheila and Eric are products of their parents' upbringing - Sheila the spoilt brat (but one with a rapidly developing social conscience) and Eric the weak, alcoholic charmer with no direction and little motivation to make anything of his life.

This makes Birling's attack on Eric all the more savage: he is furious with Eric for stealing money, and says that he has to 'cover this up as soon as I can'. Once again, he is more worried about the scandal of his son stealing money than the life of the dead girl.

The exchange between Eric and Birling is interesting. When Birling asks why Eric didn't go to him for help, Eric replies that 'you're not the kind of father a chap could go to when he's in trouble'. Birling's belief in the importance of being there for your family is blown apart - Eric was unable to go to him because he knew he'd be judged and not supported.

Birling's love of his children is conditional, the very opposite of the sort of love that nurtures. He expects them to act in a certain way, and now he finds that Eric has let him down he has nothing but scorn for him.

Again, what it keeps coming back to with Birling is the knighthood. After the dramatic exit of the Inspector, one of the first things Birling says to Eric is 'I was almost certain of a knighthood I the next honors' list -'

He goes on to say that he'll be 'the one who'll suffer' when the 'public scandal' comes out. That seems to be the only concern Birling has. Not the interrogation they've all been put through, not the death of an innocent woman. Just the public scandal. A man blinded from the truth by his own arrogant pride.

BIRLING AT THE END OF THE PLAY

In the final section of the play, it isn't Birling who questions the credibility of Inspector Goole. First Sheila, and later Gerald, call into question whether Goole was an Inspector at all. During this, Birling uses the benefit of hindsight to blame everyone for giving Goole more information than was necessary: 'the fact remains that if you hadn't talked so much, he'd really have little to go on... you allowed yourselves to be bluffed.'

Birling continually looks to shift the blame onto his children and away from himself and his wife: 'You ought to have stood up to him,' he says to Eric and Sheila. When Eric counters 'I didn't notice you standing up to him' Birling says 'What chance did I have after that?'

This is Birling the politician: a man who cannot accept responsibility for his actions and has to look to others to blame. He puts what we might call a 'spin' on the events of the evening, painting a picture of a family who gave too much away and who could have helped him to control things better. Of course, we know that is not how it was at all.

When Gerald appears, and proves that Goole was not who he said he was, Birling is ecstatic. Remember, this has nothing to do with whether or not there was an Eva/Daisy, or even whether she lived or died, but rather the fact that, if Goole wasn't a police inspector, he has no authority to make something like this public.

When it is further proven that Eva/Daisy might be more than one woman, and might not even be dead, Birling feels further let off the hook. He 'eagerly' pushes the dialogue on, to the point where they have proof that no woman died in the infirmary that night.

At this point he pours a drink for himself and Gerald and raises his glass saying 'here's to us'. This is the whole problem with men like Birling. It is always about them, and not their impact on the world around them.

Gerald has proven that no woman died, and yet as Sheila rightly says, they still acted badly towards a woman in a weaker position than them. They still took advantage of her, whoever she was.

But as far as Birling is concerned, they are all off the hook. He makes fun of the Inspector's serious 'You all helped kill her', laughs at their expressions, and shows palpable relief that his reputation is intact.

His final words are prescient (have deeper meaning based on what is about to happen). He mockingly calls Sheila and Eric 'the famous younger generation who know it all', suggesting that perhaps they don't have the understanding of the world that he has. His last word before the phone rings again - 'joke' - is interesting, because this is exactly what he sees the Inspector's visit as being - nothing more than an elaborate joke.

SYBIL BIRLING

Mrs Birling has a smaller part in the play: as much as anything because much of the play revolves around Birling's increasingly failed attempts to control the Inspector's interrogation of his family. She spends a good deal of the play off stage, and when on stage presents as a thoroughly unpleasant woman.

Why? Because to Priestley she symbolises all that is wrong with the British class system. She is patronising, elitist and thoroughly dismissive of anyone who is not in her social circle. She appears cold and unfeeling, and you sense a level of control of her family (including her husband) that comes from her privileged upbringing.

If Birling symbolises the ugly side of capitalism, his wife represents the even uglier side of 'old money': being born into wealth, with all the privileges that brings.

THE OPENING STAGE DIRECTIONS

It's interesting that Priestley highlights Mrs Birling's social superiority to her husband from the very start. I think he does this to establish just how important this is to both: Sybil Birling knows that she is of higher status to her husband, and Birling knows that it doesn't matter how successful he is, he cannot escape the fact that his wife comes from a better background than him.

This will have the effect of making Birling feel even more sensitive about background and status than he might have been were he and his wife of equal status.

Priestley also refers to Mrs Birling as 'rather cold': again, it's interesting to highlight this from the start. How much of this is her personality, and how much is her need to remain aloof and at a distance from those around her, in order to protect her status, is one to debate.

HOW MRS BIRLING INTERACTS WITH HER FAMILY

As we have mentioned before, her reaction to her husband when he lets slip his background is instructive, as it shows us just how important the rules are when it comes to being part of the upper classes.

Remember: the British class system is very much bound within a set of expectations. We commonly refer to these as **etiquette**. How to act, what to say (and how to say it), how to dress and so on. It is less important nowadays, which many would say is a shame, as there are certain elements of this code of etiquette which promote politeness and respect.

But in the world of women like Sybil Birling, these rules are used to demonstrate a separation between those who have, and those who have not. They are the governing forces of her life and the lives of her family: nothing is more important than how you act and how you are seen by others.

It is this level of control that creates a cold, distant attitude towards her family, seen in how she speaks to them. There is no warmth or kindness - it is all about judging, criticising, and controlling.

Take the first piece of advice she gives Sheila: 'When you're married you'll realise that men with important work to do sometimes have to spend nearly all their time and energy on their business.'

This is one of the rules: as the wife of an important man, you don't question, you are there as his wife whenever he has time for you. There might be a note of bitterness in her voice, but perhaps not: she simply sees this as a fact of life.

She does not want Sheila to question Gerald too much: remember our point earlier about the importance of the stable family. The woman's role is to sit at the centre of this family, to ensure it remains secure. And if a woman questions her husband too much that can unsettle things.

Mrs Birling is hyper-aware of how her children act in front of others. When Sheila calls Eric 'squiffy' (meaning drunk), Mrs Birling responds 'What an expression, Sheila! Really, the things you girls pick up these days!'

Whilst there may be a note of surprise in her voice, what she is doing here is reminding Sheila of how to act: using slang like 'squiffy' is not the sort of language a girl like Sheila should be using. By referring to 'you girls' and 'these days' she is commenting on how the world is changing and how the correct way to speak and act is being lost.

As the play develops, we sense an increasing disconnection between Mrs Birling and her children: she doesn't understand them, and they feel little affection towards her.

When Birling mentions that the marriage will bring him closer to his rival Crofts Limited, Mrs Birling is the first to comment 'Now, Arthur, I don't think you ought to talk business on an occasion like this'. She is continually asserting the 'rules of the game', like a referee, always trying to keep the conversation within the bounds of decency. Must be pretty exhausting for her, don't you think?

HOW MRS BIRLING FIRST RESPONDS TO THE INSPECTOR

Once she exits in Act 1, Mrs Birling doesn't return until Act 2 is well underway. By this time, a number of new rules have been established, and a lot of information has been disclosed that she has no idea about.

So, when she comes back in and acts in her usual way, she is in for a big surprise. It is fascinating to watch her social superiority fail her completely, and how utterly out of her depth she is. Without having etiquette to fall back on she is lost. It's a bit like someone knowing the rules of rugby really well and walking into a game of football and picking up the ball...

She enters a room filled with tension utterly oblivious to anything that has just been said. Priestley, in his stage directions, refers to Mrs Birling entering as 'social': she puts on her usual act, to welcome the Inspector but tell him 'I don't think we can help you much.'

She uses a more informal tone to attempt to assert her social superiority over the Inspector - 'I'm Mrs Birling, y'know' - but of course this has no effect whatsoever on the man. It's interesting to note Sheila's reaction to Mrs Birling's easygoing attitude to the Inspector: 'No - mother - please!'. Sheila knows this is a mistake - the Inspector will tear this attitude apart.

In many ways Sheila mirrors our own response - we are thinking *noooo, Mrs Birling - don't go there! You have no idea who this man is or what he's capable of!* and so on. We can see that this is a car crash waiting to happen, but Mrs Birling won't be told. Like her husband she is too stuffed full of pride to listen to others.

As before, she tries to control the situation, suggesting to Sheila that she go to bed 'and forget about this absurd business'. However, Sheila ignores her, which is the first sign that Mrs Birling has 'lost the room'.

When Sheila contradicts her mother, Mrs Birling becomes annoyed. She simply isn't listening to Sheila when she says 'You mustn't try to build up a kind of wall between us and that girl'. On more than one occasion Mrs Birling says 'I don't understand'. This is true: she isn't being awkward. She is totally out of her depth and has no idea of the seriousness of what is going on.

The problem is that she has no interest in Eva Smith's life or death. To her, Eva is one of the 'little people', not worthy of time or attention. She does not yet realise how caught up her family is in this woman's death: as far as she is concerned, this is a waste of her time.

She despises men like the Inspector who act as if they have more status than they deserve. And so when Sheila tries to stop her, Mrs Birling ignores her. She has spent her life having people listen to her and agree with her - so is sure that this man will soon realise who she is and change his tune.

But, like her husband, she is about to have a rude awakening.

The first realisation comes when Sheila tells her mother about Eric's drinking problem. 'We really must stop these silly pretences,' Sheila says. 'He's been steadily drinking too much for the last two years.'

In the stage directions, Priestley tells us that Mrs Birling is 'staggered' by this. Her first response is to say 'It isn't true. You know him Gerald - and you're a man - you must know it isn't true.'

Bang - the first pretence is knocked down, and Mrs Birling finds it hard to believe. These are the walls that Sheila refers to, those artificial barriers that separate people like the Birlings from the real world. It is impossible that a well-bred young man like Eric could have a drink problem. But of course when your arrogant pride blinds you from the truth, anything is possible even if you're unaware of it.

As we have already seen, this is the Inspector's role. To take each of the family's prejudices and knock them down by holding them up to inspection in the cold light of day. We can almost see the Inspector less in the more traditional police sense, and more as a man who opens up the truth for inspection by everyone present - a bit like a surgeon opens up a body. Some might learn, others might not, but the truth has to be revealed in all its ugliness if any of them have a hope of learning.

It doesn't take a genius to work out the Mrs Birling will not be one of those who learns from this, which is all rather frustrating and depressing for the likes of Sheila. And I guess writers like Priestley, who saw the horrors of the First World War first hand, then had to live through the whole ordeal a second time when no one seemed to learn the lessons of the Great War.

MRS BIRLING'S INTERROGATION

Towards the end of Act 2, the Inspector moves on to the questioning of Mrs Birling. Based on what we've seen of her so far, we are probably expecting her to be a tough nut to crack. But how the Inspector deals with her is a brilliant piece of manipulation (as it has been with the others in the family).

You see, what the Inspector continually does is **use each character's own prejudices and faults against them**. With Mr Birling, it was his arrogant pride and belief that keeping costs low is more important than the lives he is responsible for as an employer. With Sheila, it was her naivety and her insecurity which resulted in her jealous reaction to Eva's beauty. With Gerald it was his view of himself as the saviour of a weak, needy woman.

But with Mrs Birling, it is all about her rigid adherence to the code of etiquette: so less about any personal qualities and more about the rules within which she lives her life. She turns Eva/Daisy away because she does not play the role of pathetic, vulnerable, grateful girl well enough.

Eva refers initially to herself as 'Mrs Birling', which Mrs Birling sees as a 'piece of gross impertinence': of course, we know that this was probably because Eva had recently had a relationship with Eric and not because she was deliberately being impertinent, but to Mrs Birling there can only be one reason.

Mrs Birling continually asserts that Eva 'had only herself to blame' for her unpleasant death, which is a pretty terrible thing to say! She admits that it was her intervention that refused Eva help when she needed it most, simply because she 'didn't like her manner'.

Unlike the other characters, it would appear that Mrs Birling has no intention of admitting fault. As far as she is concerned, she considers she did her 'duty' in refusing the girl, and believes she has done 'nothing wrong'.

Even when the Inspector informs them that Eva was pregnant, Mrs Birling does not climb down from her perch. 'I'll tell you what I told her,' she says. 'Go and look for the father of the child. It's his responsibility.'

As we've explored earlier, Mrs Birling's attitude to women like Eva is worth examining in the light of everything we've learnt about her so far. She says of Eva 'She was giving herself ridiculous airs. She was claiming elaborate fine feelings and scruples that were simply absurd in a girl in her position.'

Remember what we've said about this so far? This sense of 'us and them', which ultimately led to the deaths of more than six million Jews in the concentration camps of Nazi Germany? It starts like this: with women like Mrs Birling saying that girls like Eva Smith cannot feel in the same way as people of a higher class. That they are somehow less human, less able to experience a range of emotions.

It is only when Mrs Birling begins to describe the 'young man' who got Eva pregnant that the penny starts to drop, both for us and for Sheila.

After she repeatedly blames this man for Eva's predicament - 'I blame the young man who was the father of the child she was going to have' - Sheila suddenly realises who this man was. She says 'Mother - stop - stop!', as it becomes clear to her that this man is in fact Eric.

But not Mrs Birling - oh no. She is on a self-righteous roll and isn't going to let this horrible little man ruin her evening. Talk about digging a hole for yourself!

And then - her world falls apart. When the Inspector says he is waiting for that very man, the stage directions tell us just how Mrs

Birling feels. She takes 'two steps to Sheila, to Inspector…crosses to L chair, ready to collapse.'

She doesn't know where to go. She is totally lost. The hole she has just dug has opened up and swallowed her.

MRS BIRLING IN ACT 3

We ended Act 2 with the arrival of Eric. It's interesting to see how Mrs Birling changes now she knows the truth. In many way it is the most human we see her in the play. She continually says that she cannot believe it, and utters the occasional 'Eric, how could you!' Unsurprising based on what she has just found out.

The scene builds to a climax when Eric turns on her saying 'you killed them both' (referring to Eva and her unborn child). Mrs Birling's response - 'No, Eric - please - I didn't know - I didn't understand!' - says it all: she has no understanding of how the world works and how to live a good life. She has been so caught up in her own privileged bubble that shc has failed to see her family falling apart under her nose. Either failed to see, or didn't want to see. We sense some denial in her tone.

However, when the Inspector leaves and the truth of the hoax begins to be uncovered, we see the old Mrs Birling resurface. She 'triumphantly' says 'Didnt I tell you? Didn't I say I couldn't image a real police inspector talking like that to us?' She has to shift everything back to her, seemingly already forgetting the revelation about her son.

She contines in the same way, taking the moral high ground in saying that she 'was the only one of you who didn't give in to him.' As if not backing down when accused of sending a young girl to her death is a good thing. It shows how her principles are more important than another person's life: two people's to be precise.

It is her belief that they should all now 'behave sensibly' the pushes Eric over the edge. As far as Mrs Birling is concerned, the only important thing is to act in the proper way, discussing 'this business' quietly and sensibly 'and decide if there's anything to be done about it.' You have to admire her ability to compose herself and look ahead, even if it shows her in a pretty terrible light.

Like Birling, the only thing she is interested in is saving face. Not her children, and certainly not Eva/Daisy. Just herself and her position in society. She'd probably throw her whole family under the bus if it saved her skin.

Towards the end of the Act, when Gerald finally reveals that no girl died in the infirmary, Mrs Birling thanks him in an interesting way: 'I must say, Gerald, you've argued this very cleverly'. Like a lawyer, Gerald has managed to approach the events of the evening in a clinical, objective way, and has shown the Inspector to be a hoax.

To the Birlings, this is all that matters - not anything that led to these accusations, but simply the fact that Goole was not real. What any of the family did can be dealt with internally - as long as it doesn't leak out they will be fine. As we've seen before, it shows them for who they really are - people who only care about themselves and their place in society. Status above human life, above family. Above everything.

Mrs Birling is a classic example of someone for whom position is all. This position has come both from her birth and upbringing, but also the carefully crafted place she has carved for herself in Brumley society. She can let nothing get in the way of that.

But, as the play closes with the revelation that there has indeed been a girl found dead having drunk disinfectant, we realise that the sand upon which she has built this place is soon to give way and bury her.

And as far as Priestley is concerned, it serves her right.

SHEILA BIRLING

Sheila is the character who goes on the biggest journey. She begins as a rather spoilt, childish girl and ends as a young woman with a maturing aspect on the world, an understanding of the effect she has on others, and a realisation that her fiance and parents are not who she thought they were.

She represents the sort of people that Priestley mosts wants to change through this play: young, impressionable, who perhaps have not stopped to consider that every action as its consequences. Above all, Priestley wants to guard against the sort of complacent thinking that got the world into the mess it had only just come out of. Don't accept things as they are. Protest, seek change, look for a better way to live.

Interestingly, what came out of these postwar debates was a youth culture that became increasingly militant and demanded further and further change. The civil rights movement, feminism, the counter-culture of the 1960s - all of them came after the Second World War, and profoundly shaped the world we live in today. I'm sure Priestley would be pleased to see that it was the literature of protest like his play that helped to start that debate off.

THE OPENING STAGE DIRECTIONS

As with the other characters, we gain a little understanding of Sheila through Priestley's short description of her. Priestley describes her as 'a pretty girl in her early twenties, very pleased with life and rather excited.'

We can read a lot into this. She is referred to as 'a pretty girl', which immediately makes her seem childlike. This is further emphasised by her being 'excited': she would come across as quite naive, perhaps a little giddy, and full of confidence.

It is the fact that she is 'pleased with herself' which tells us the most about her. She knows she is lucky - she has a solid family, money, and a handsome man who wants to marry her. Of course, we will soon see the cracks in this forming, but from the opening we sense a young woman who knows she has it good, and as far as she is concerned this is how it should be.

Like her parents and Gerald, there is an arrogance in her that the Inspector will very soon tear apart.

OUR FIRST IMPRESSIONS OF SHEILA

We learn a lot from Sheila from the first thing she says to Gerald. When Gerald tells Birling that he doesn't know much about port, Sheila says 'I should jolly well think so, Gerald.' Priestley gives us the stage directions 'Gaily, possessively' indicating how she says this.

First of all, she is a little passive aggressive here: in other words, masking a more serious, negative intention with a light-hearted tone of voice. She is possessive of Gerald, not wanting him to turn into 'one of these purple-faced old men'. We see her wanting to control Gerald from the start, probably in the way she sees her mother subtly controlling Birling.

There is a definite tension in the way she says 'with mock aggressive-ness' 'Just you object!' when Birling says he is treating Gerald like one of the family. This tension continues when Sheila 'half serious, half playful' questions where Gerald was 'all last summer when you never came near me'.

Of course, we will soon find out where he was, but for now what we can see is an anxiety in Sheila, but one she is trying to cover up with humour. Sheila is doing her best to play the part of the dutiful fiancee, but there are questions she has which are clearly causing her some worry, even if she tries on the surface not to be too direct in challenging Gerald.

When Mrs Birling says that Sheila will have to 'get used to' Gerald sometimes having to spend a lot of time at work, Sheila says 'I don't believe I will.' She believes, perhaps naively, that she will maintain a sense of individuality and be able to dictate the terms of her marriage to Gerald. What Mrs Birling seems to be saying is that this is doubtful - Sheila will have to get used to sometimes coming second to Gerald's work.

What we see here is a clash between a more traditional view of marriage, shown by Mrs Birling, and a more modern, equal version, shown by Sheila. What Sheila wants is to be a proper partner in this marriage, not a silent, passive woman who has to sit waiting for her husband to come home, wondering where he is and what he is doing but not being able to question.

There is another reason why setting the play in 1912 is interesting: the Women's Social and Political Union was founded by Emmeline Pankhurst in 1903, demanding the vote for women. By 1912, what were now known as Suffragettes were taking more direct action, such as chaining themselves to railings, setting fire to post boxes, smashing windows, and occasionally setting off bombs.

It might well be that Sheila has been inspired by these women, and believes it important for her to assert herself and not merely be seen as Mrs Gerald Croft. No mention is made of women's suffrage in the play, but the actions of Eva Smith at Birling's company suggest a desire for a fairer world.

Whilst she may in part wish to retain her individuality, she reverts to the more stereotypical young girl when Gerald presents the engage-

ment ring. She is 'excited', saying 'Oh - it's wonderful! L
mummy - Isn't it a beauty? Oh - darling - ' This materialistic sy
of the intended marriage shows the more superficial side of Sheila:
she loves that Gerald has clearly bought her a very expensive ring.

At this point she refers to her parents as 'mummy' and 'daddy': this
reminds us of her age, and how she still feels like their little girl. By
the end of the play this has changed dramatically, but for now she is
happy to play the role of dutiful daughter.

SHEILA'S FIRST REACTION TO THE INSPECTOR

When Sheila reappears towards the end of Act 1, Birling's first
response is to remove her from the scene. He says 'Nothing to do
with you, Sheila. Run along', as one would to a child. Birling still
sees Sheila as his little girl and wants to protect her from the grim
reality that the Inspector has brought into the evening.

When she discovers the reason for the Inspector's presence in the
house her first response is unsurprising based on what we have
learned about her so far: 'I've been so happy tonight. Oh, I wish
you hadn't told me.' She doesn't want this grim reality interfering
with her good mood. This is a conditioned, selfish reaction, a desire
to keep everything as it was before and not allow anything to
destroy it.

But that, as we very well know, is the Inspector's job. To break these
people apart and see if there is anything worth rebuilding.

SHEILA IS QUESTIONED BY THE INSPECTOR

Because she has not been in the room during Birling's interrogation,
Sheila doesn't yet know the Inspector's approach. She doesn't appre-
ciate his ability to lead each of them to pretty well admit their guilt
without realising it.

So, when the Inspector begins to talk about a woman who has was
dismissed from Milward's, Sheila suspects nothing. It is only when
she realises that Eva was dismissed due to a customer complaint,

and then sees her photograph, that Sheila realises her role in the girl's death.

Her reaction, to give a 'half stifled sob' before running out of the room, is exactly the reaction we'd expect from a girl like Sheila. Birling's response, to ask the Inspector why he would want to 'go upsetting a child like that' is also what we'd expect from him.

No surprises that a girl who'd spent her life wrapped in cotton wool and treated like a child reacts by running from the room. It will only be when she returns that we see a different Sheila emerging from all this.

Sheila returns quite quickly. What is notable about her response is that she immediately blames herself: 'So I'm responsible?' She can see that it was her fault she got 'in a furious temper' with Eva for seeming to smile at a colleague when Sheila was trying on a dress that she knew didn't suit her. Sheila admits that Eva's looks 'didn't make it any better': she lashed out at the girl because the dress would have suited Eva better than Sheila.

Remember what we've been exploring about how the Inspector uses each character's faults against them, to explode their prejudices and hopefully make them face the ugly truth of their lives?

Here's Sheila's, plain and simple. Sheila is a pretty girl, we know that from the stage directions: but she is also a competitive girl with a bit of a possessive streak - again, we've seen that with the opening conversation with Gerald. She won't like anyone looking better than her, least of all a common shop girl.

She felt humiliated by what happened in the shop and used her status to have Eva fired, threatening the manager that they would close their account unless he did as she asked. Her jealousy at Eva's looks motivated her to act in a terrible way, and now she feels ashamed.

As she perceptively says, 'If she'd been some miserable plain little creature, I don't suppose I'd have done it.' Time and again throughout the play, Eva's good looks have led to her downfall.

THE END OF ACT 1: SHEILA AND GERALD TALK

This is the only time in the play we get a 'two-hander' - two people only on stage. During this, Sheila makes it clear she knows that Gerald has had a relationship with Eva/Daisy. He tries to hide it but she is too perceptive and sees through him.

In fact, she doesn't even need him to answer her questions - she knows the answer already. This is probably because she had an inkling that he might be having an affair even before this evening: her rather passive aggressive approach to Gerald from the start gave it away.

What is more interesting about the end of Act 1 is how Sheila responds when Gerald asks her not to say anything to the Inspector: 'Why, you fool - he knows! Of course he knows.' Sheila has already worked out that this man knows a lot more than any of them realise, and that his approach is to make them admit to themselves how appallingly they've behaved and how they are all responsible for a young woman's death.

She understands the rules of the game, which only adds to her anxiety when she sees her mother getting it totally wrong later. More on this shortly.

ACT 2 - SHEILA THE 'HYSTERICAL' GIRL

Gerald kicks things off by trying to have Sheila removed from the room. His euphemism - 'she's had a long exciting and tiring day' - is quickly picked up on by Sheila as meaning that she is 'hysterical'. It's worth spending a few moments on this word, as it's an important one:

It's actually a pretty new word in the context of 1912: the word **hysteria** actually comes from the ancient Greek word for the female uterus: you may have heard of an operation called a hysterectomy, which is the removal of the uterus.

For most of the 19th Century (so the decades leading up to the time in which the play is set) hysteria was seen as a disorder of the uterus, therefore a female-only condition. Nowadays we see hysteria as a mental condition, not a physical one, but at the start of the 20th Century many still believed that women were naturally more irrational and emotional and that this was due to their physical differences to men.

By referring to Sheila as hysterical, Gerald is seeking to control her through her sexuality. We see this a lot in history: men using women's bodies against them.

There is an interesting discussion between the Inspector and Gerald over femininity at this point, which I think is worth mentioning as it compares Sheila to Eva. Gerald suggests that Sheila shouldn't be exposed to his ugly truth because 'It'd bound to be unpleasant and disturbing.' The Inspector asks whether Gerald believes that women should be protected from such things. When Gerald agrees, the Inspector says 'Well, we know one young woman who wasn't, don't we?'

This shows the double standard within which men like Gerald and Eric operate. They are quite happy to protect women from their own social class, but when it comes to those from a lower class they are not worth protecting. Yes, on the surface it would seem that both Gerald and Eric had feelings for Eva/Daisy, but they both knew the relationship wouldn't last and that ultimately they were only in it for the physical side.

Just before the arrival of Mrs Birling, we can see Sheila already questioning the Inspector's methods. She begins by saying 'I don't understand about you?' and then follows with 'I don't know much about police inspectors - but the ones I have met weren't a bit like you.' This is lost a little with the arrival of Mrs Birling, but it is interesting to note that Sheila is the only one who questions the Inspector there and then.

SHEILA TRIES TO STOP HER MOTHER FROM DIGGING A BIG HOLE

As we've seen with our analysis of Mrs Birling, Sheila does her best to stop her mother from saying too much and getting herself into trouble. Sheila understands the Inspector's methods and can see from the very start how her mother will get herself into hot water if she continues in the same arrogant, blase way with him.

'I know it sounds silly,' Sheila says. 'You see, I feel you're beginning all wrong…We all started like that…' Sheila has already learnt from the mistakes Birling, Gerald and she made, and doesn't want to see her mother go down the same round. Fat chance, Sheila - don't you know your mother by now?

Sheila's comment about the 'wall' is possibly the most important line in the play: 'You mustn't build up a kind of wall between us and that girl. If you do, then the Inspector will just break it down.'

It is a deeply perceptive thing to say: the Birlings, as a moneyed, upper middle class family, have built an emotional wall between themselves and the little people, the commoners like Eva/Daisy. The Inspector's job is to break this down, to make them see Eva as a human being, flesh and blood just like them, wanting happiness and feeling pain in the same way they do.

Sheila gets it from the very start, but Mrs Birling's lesson will have to be much harder, as her wall is much higher and much thicker. And probably has razor wire on the top. And machine gun turrets. You get the idea.

Sheila knows that the Inspector will break it down: she is in no doubt that he has the tools to do so. But Mrs Birling, caught as she is inside her arrogance and pride, either does not, or cannot see this. Perhaps she just isn't as clever as Sheila. She certainly comes across as being pretty ignorant.

You have to feel for Sheila at this point in the play. She's just found out that she was partly responsible for a young woman's death, is about to have confirmed that her fiance had been a bad boy, and now she's watching her mother humiliate herself without realising.

Going back to the football analogy I introduced earlier, Sheila must feel like she's playing a football match but is the only one who actually knows the rules. The others of her family are doing crazy things like picking up the ball and kicking it into their own goal, and it doesn't matter how much she tries to tell them they are doing it all wrong, they carry on blindly.

Time and again she tells her mother to 'stop', but Mrs Birling marches on regardless.

When Mr Birling says to the Inspector 'I don't propose to give you any more rope', Sheila 'wildly' replies 'No, he's giving us rope - so that we'll hang ourselves!' The Inspector is simply allowing them to speak, and through their own words they are admitting guilt without him doing much at all.

DURING GERALD'S INTERROGATION

There is a certain amount of bitterness in Sheila's voice during Gerald's admittance that he had an affair with Daisy Renton. 'You were the wonderful fairy prince. You must have adored it,' she says to him. When Gerald replies 'All right - I did. Nearly every man would have done,' Sheila says 'That's probably the best thing you've said tonight. At least it's honest.'

All Sheila now wants is total honesty from those around her. She can see that failing to be honest, to own up to individual responsibilty for Eva/Daisy's death, will only make it worse for them all in the end. She can see that the world around her has been built on lies, and she is actually grateful to Gerald for being honest, even if the truth is painful for her.

When Sheila hands back the engagement ring, she once again sums up the situation with precision. 'You and I aren't the same people who sat down to dinner here. We'd have to start all over again, getting to know each other - '.

What the Inspector has done is broken apart the pretence upon which they had previously built there seemingly 'perfect' relationship, and if there is any hope of it surviving they have to start from the beginning, to build a firmer foundation, not one built on sand.

Interestingly, when Birling tries to interrupt - 'you must understand that a lot of young men' - Sheila is having none of it: 'Don't interfere…Gerald knows what I mean, and you apparently don't.'

As far as Birling is concerned, what Gerald did is pretty normal. But for Sheila this is something far more profound. She won't be in a marriage built around lies. She expects honesty, and has the strength of character to not slam the door completely on Gerald.

You have to hand it to her: she is coming out of this looking pretty good. Not because she was any less guilty of what happened to Eva/Daisy, but because she can see that only total honesty will enable her to escape this with a hope of moving forward.

DURING MRS BIRLING'S INTERROGATION

Sheila acts almost like the Inspector's assistant during Mrs Birling's questioning, saying things like 'Go on, mother, you may as well admit it' and 'can't you see… you're making it worse?' She just wants her mother to admit to her part in the girl's death and show some remorse.

Of course, and as we've mentioned earlier, it's Sheila who suddenly realises that Eva's child is Eric's. 'With sudden alarm' she says 'Mother - stop - stop!… don't you see?'

Nope, Mrs Birling doesn't, not straight away. It takes a few more clues from the Inspector before she realises where this conversation has led to. She's not only kicked the ball into her own net; she's taken a knife and stabbed a big hole in it. As I said, poor Sheila. You can't choose your family!

ACT 3: ADJUSTING FAMILY RELATIONSHIPS

Even though Sheila's intentions are one hundred percent decent, her parents cannot see this. When she explains to Eric why she told their mother about his drinking ('I only told her tonight because I knew that everything was coming out') Mrs Birling says 'I simply cannot understand your attitude' and Birling adds 'If you had any sense of loyalty'.

For the Birlings, being loyal to your family seems to be more important than being honest and open. However, this is pretty hypocritical, as they're quite prepared to throw Eric under the bus when he later admits to stealing money.

Their own reputation is more important than their children. But by now that probably doesn't surprise us.

The Inspector interrupts saying 'there'll be plenty of time when I'm gone for you all to adjust your family relationships'. You'd hope that was the case, but something about the Birlings suggest they know what the relationship should be, and that won't change.

They certainly won't look at Sheila with any more respect, even though she deserves a good deal more. They don't want her questioning them and their authority: remember our point earlier about the stability of the family being at the centre of a stable society.

THE INSPECTOR LEAVES

As we've noted before, the moments after the Inspector leaves tell us a lot about each character. For Sheila, it's all about her showing her frustration that none of her family 'seem to have learnt anything'. That's why the Inspector was there; to hold a mirror up to each family member so they could see who they really were, and learn from what they saw.

But as we've said, that hasn't really happened.

When Sheila begins to question whether the Inspector was genuine, Birling says 'if he wasn't, it matters a devil of a lot. It makes all the difference.' Sheila disagrees: 'it doesn't to me - and it oughtn't to you either.'

It's not about how genuine Goole was, but what he made them reveal about themselves: 'if all that's come out tonight is true, then it doesn't much matter who it was made us confess?…it's what we did that's important.'

Of course, Eric agrees with her, but their parents are dead set on separating the acts from the person who made them admit to what they did. What Sheila is trying to make them realise is that it doesn't matter who made them confess: it takes nothing away from what they did.

We can see though that her parents aren't going to change their tune - as far as they are concerned, what they did is far less important than the 'public scandal' that would come out were Goole to have been a real inspector.

Sheila 'bitterly' says 'I suppose we're all nice people now.' Her frustration at her family's inability to learn is turning into the bitter realisation that nothing has changed: she might have hoped that her parents would have seen the light, learnt something about themselves and become better people. But as the play nears its end, she understands that this is not going to happen: you can't teach an old dog new tricks. Particularly if the old dog is a bigot.

You can sense in her tone of voice that she feels defeated. The only person who she can see has been affected by it is Eric, but their parents don't want to listen so they are on their own.

After they discover the fact that there is no dead girl, the Birlings are massively relieved. However, Sheila cannot celebrate. As she rightly says, 'Everything we said happened really had happened. If it didn't end tragically, that's lucky for us.' The visit of Goole was there as a warning to them, to change their ways lest they make an even bigger mistake in future.

Sheila is 'frightened' by how her parents are acting: she knows that this cannot be laughed off as a big joke. This was serious, a forensic examination of their prejudices, a chance for them to understand how their selfish, materialistic lives had potentially impacted on one person.

The final stage direction, once they hear that a girl really has died, is interesting. Sheila 'faces the door' and then 'rises'. She is ready for the real inspector; in fact she was probably expecting this to happen.

Sheila has been created by Priestley to show us that the younger generation can change, indeed want to change. However, they feel held back by the older generation's prejudices and arrogant belief that they know better. However, like the fact that the First World War clearly didn't teach the world a big enough lesson, the revelation of the real dead girl is a little like the Second World War. We get the feeling that this time round it will be a lot worse.

ERIC BIRLING

Whilst Eric has a smaller part to play, he is no less an interesting character because of it. Unlike Sheila, he plays a passive part throughout, reacting to what is happening around him but taking little active interest in the proceedings. It is only at the end of the play, when his truth comes out, that we see how damaged he is by his parents' attitudes towards him and towards life in general.

Eric is a troubled young man who has over the last few years begun to drink heavily, probably to mask his unhappiness. His parents have either been ignorant of his drinking problem or have been in denial. He comes across as a deeply sensitive young man who is ill-suited to his father's aggressive approach to business. We sense that his father is disappointed in him, and sees in Gerald more the son he wishes he'd had.

THE OPENING STAGE DIRECTIONS

Eric is described as 'not quite at ease, half shy, half assertive.' He feels out of place in this gathering, and has used alcohol to mask his discomfort. This is probably why he seems contradictory, both shy and assertive, as the alcohol will give him a sort of false confidence.

OUR FIRST IMPRESSIONS

Eric says little in Act 1, and then disappears for the middle part of the play. His first action in the play is to laugh at Sheila's mock serious warning to Gerald to 'be careful' about not spending too much time away from home.

Sheila responds 'severely' to Eric, asking him 'what's the joke?' Eric's reply ('I don't know - I just suddenly felt I had to laugh') acts as a sort of pressure valve, releasing the tension that is clearly in the room.

Eric's sensitivity is demonstrated here in his laughter: he senses a tension growing and has to release his own anxiety through laughter. It probably isn't that he finds what Sheila has said funny, but more the fact that he probably can't imagine Sheila being a quiet, stay at home wife who never questions her husband's activities.

We can see Eric's youthful honesty when he 'not too rudely' suggests to his father that he doesn't make a speech, when Birling complains that speechmaking is more difficult with a smaller audience.

Unlike his parents, Eric is an open book, happy to speak his mind but not in such a way that causes offence. He is probably still too much in his father's shadow to openly challenge him: but not for much longer.

ERIC'S RESPONSE TO BIRLING'S SPEECH

Eric clearly wishes to question some of his father's assertions over how Gerald and Sheila will be marrying 'at a very good time'. 'What about war?' Eric asks, to which Birling then responds 'don't interrupt'. Birling is not interested in his son's worries about the state of the world, or anything that challenges his belief that things will only get better for people like the Birlings.

It's worth spending a few moments looking at the world in 1912. Whilst the First World War would not begin until

July/August 1914, plenty was happening in the world leading up to that point, including wars across Eastern Europe.

During 1912 and 1913, there were wars across the Balkans (the area comprising of Albania, Bulgaria, Bosnia, Kosovo, Macedonia and Montenegro, and parts of Croatia, Serbia and Slovenia). This led to an increase in Russian power across Europe, creating an imbalance of power which set in process a chain of events that would eventually lead to the First World War.

Eric then is right to question his father, as the world was not a stable place in 1912. Of course for men like Birling they could not believe that some war being fought thousands of miles away would ever affect them. This shows their ignorance and a rather arrogant, colonial attitude to the world. This attitude would soon come back to bite those in authority.

DURING BIRLING'S INTERROGATION

When Eric hears that Birling sacked Eva when she complained about low pay, Eric says 'Why shouldn't they try for high wages? We try for the highest possible prices.'

This is an important point, and underpins Eric's belief that everyone should be given the chance to better themselves. And he is right: why shouldn't Eva do exactly what Birling does, aim for the maximum amount of return on her time investment in Birling's business?

Of course, as far as the likes of Birling is concerned, this is naive nonsense: men like Birling are the ones who make these sorts of decisions - it is not for the powerless like Eva to decide how much they are paid.

Birling's argument - 'if they didn't like those rates, they could go and work somewhere else' - is questioned by Eric: 'It isn't if you can't go and work somewhere else'. Birling believes in a free market - workers can move on if they don't like the pay and conditions of their current employment. But as Eric rightly says, it's not as easy as that. There have to be jobs to go to.

ALONE WITH GERALD AND THE INSPECTOR

There is a short section when Eric and Gerald are alone with the Inspector, when Birling exits and before Sheila enters. Eric immediately appears nervous: he and Gerald 'exchange uneasy glances' and when the Inspector refuses to show them the photograph of Eva Eric suddenly burst out 'Look here, I've had enough of this... I'm sorry - but you see - we were having a little party - and I've had a few drinks...and I've got a headache - and as I'm only in the way here - I think I'd better turn in.'

Why does he do this, and why is he so nervous? Probably because the Inspector has just said to Gerald 'If you've anything to tell me, you'll have an opportunity of doing it soon.' Perhaps Eric realises already that the Inspector is not at the house only to speak to Birling. There is more at stake here, and Eric probably begins to wonder what role he might have played. After all, it is probably fair to say that his relationship with Eva/Daisy wouldn't have been his first and last.

THIRD ACT INTERROGATION

At the end of Act 2, Eric reappears, having been offstage for the whole of the Act. During this time he has realised that the Inspector has known all along that he was responsible for getting Eva pregnant: like Sheila, he understands early on what is happening.

His first words in Act 3 - 'You know, don't you?' - begin a shift in Eric's attitude towards his family. Now that his truth is out he can show them how bitter and angry he feels. He calls his sister a 'little sneak' which is quite an immature thing to say, but also demonstrates the code of loyalty expected of the family. This is of course backed up when Birling tells Sheila she has no 'sense of loyalty'.

Interestingly, Eric does not even try to hide the truth from the Inspector. By now he knows that the man has all the facts anyway, so he is giving the answers as much for his family and for himself as for the Inspector.

And this is the whole point. What the Inspector is trying to achieve with all of them. He's not interrogating these people so that he learns the truth. His role is to open them up to themselves and each other. To make them finally confront who they really are. For Sheila and Eric, and initially for Gerald (although he reverts in Act 3), the Inspector achieves what he set out to do. For Birling and his wife the effect is a little different.

So, the inspection that Goole undertakes isn't so that he has the answers he needs in order to prosecute. *He wants the family to inspect themselves*: and this is exactly what Eric now does.

Notice how emotionless Eric now is: previously, we have seen quite a 'hot and cold' character, one who lives on his emotions, at odds with his rather cold, clinical parents. Now he answers the questions calmly without any real emotion. This is the Inspector stripping that away from him, showing the ugly truth.

At one point Eric says 'Oh - my God! How stupid it all is!' Now that he is retelling these events in an objective way he can see them for what they really are: nothing more than a selfish young man looking for a good time and using a weak woman for his own pleasure.

Throughout the interrogation, as Eric admits to stealing money from his father's business in order to help Eva out, we sense his building anger towards his family. This isn't helped by his father's aggressive attitude towards him.

It is when he finds out that his mother turned Eva away that the anger really shows itself. It is as if this has been waiting to come out for years, but Eric has masked it with alcohol. Remember: the

Inspector's role is to strip away the layers of lies and denials, the things that stop this family from learning, growing, and leading decent lives. Eric's anger at his parents has been just beneath the surface for years, but through the Inspector's skilled questioning all is soon to come out.

Eric is now 'nearly at breaking point', and shouts at his mother 'you killed her…you killed them both! Damn you!' At this point he is 'almost threatening her', and the truth finally emerges: 'You don't understand anything - you never did. You never tried - you - '

Notice how many times we see dashes with Eric's speech. It is as if he can't quite think of the right words to say, or is so emotional that his mind isn't clear and the words tumble out without any particular order. This is Eric at his most raw and broken. But this is exactly where the Inspector wants him, so that he can now begin to rebuild his life.

AFTER THE INSPECTOR LEAVES

When the Inspector leaves we can see that the relationship between Eric and his parents has utterly changed. There is no more respect: Eric says 'I don't care now' and 'What does it matter now whether they give you a knighthood or not?' He is no longer interested in their opinion, and sees them for who they really are. And he is disgusted by them.

Once again Eric shows a perceptivity that is lacking in every other character but Sheila. When Sheila says 'it's what we did that's important - and not whether a man is a Police Inspector or not', Eric replies 'He was our Police Inspector, all right.' Eric gets it - he can see that it doesn't matter how official this man might have been - his role was to force each family member to inspect themselves, to see their ugly truth and hopefully force a change.

As the play draws to its conclusion, Eric echoes Sheila's words when he says 'It's still the same rotten story whether its told to a Police Inspector or to somebody else.'

Eric says little more as the play concludes. When it is discovered that there was no dead girl in the hospital, the only words he utters are to remind Sheila that he is not relieved unlike the others. For him and his sister, things aren't as they were before, and never will be. They were all guilty of treating a woman badly, and whether or not it lead to her death is irrelevant. For Eric, like Sheila, it is the act, and not the result, that is most important.

GERALD CROFT

Gerald is the ambitious, somewhat arrogant son of Sir George Croft, Birling's business rival. Gerald swings from an open acceptance of his wrongdoing when questioned by the Inspector, to relief at the end of the play that Goole was in fact a hoax. Gerald's final words in the play ('Everything's all right now') show us how little he has learnt and how much like Birling he actually is.

THE OPENING STAGE DIRECTIONS

Gerald is described as 'rather too many to be a dandy, but very much the easy well-bred young-man-about-town'. There is a confidence to him which comes from being the son of a wealthy, influential man. If we compare him to Eric we can see the difference. We sense that Gerald has come from a family who are not striving to be wealthier, because they have already made it and have much less to prove. He is very different to Eric, who has been brought up in a much less emotionally secure environment.

GERALD PLAYING THE ROLE OF THE FUTURE SON IN LAW

From the opening of the play we can see Gerald playing the game. He comments modestly about his lack of knowledge about port, agrees that the meal was 'first class', and is keen to assure Sheila that he will be careful not to spend too much time at work. He continually tries to make a good impression, agreeing with what the Birlings say and attempting to show everyone how much he loves Sheila.

When he produces the ring case, Sheila's response is as he had hoped. You sense that everything is working out nicely for Gerald, just as it has more than likely done all his life. He has money, influence through his father, and is now engaged to a beautiful woman. What could possibly go wrong?

GERALD AND BIRLING SPEAK ALONE

However, all is not necessarily perfect. When the others leave the room, Birling suggests to Gerald that his mother, Lady Croft, 'feels you might have done better for yourself socially' - in other words, Gerald's mother doesn't feel that Sheila is the right social class for him.

Gerald seems embarrassed by this, and 'begins to murmur some dissent', but he knows what Birling is talking about. Lady Croft 'comes from an old country family - landed people and so-forth - and so it's only natural.'

It's worth spending a few moments on what Birling says here, as it backs up a lot of what we've so far been exploring about class. Lady Croft is from the upper classes. Like Mrs Birling, she has inherited wealth and status, rather than self-made wealth like Birling. 'Landed people' means those who inherit their titles, such as Lord and Lady.

What is interesting is that Birling uses the word 'natural'. For him, having the status that comes from inheriting wealth and titles is part of the natural order of things, therefore should not be questioned. He also mentions the 'country', the natural home of the upper classes. The city, which we sense is very much Birling's home, is a symbol of middle class progress.

Birling can do nothing to change the fact that he does not come from this world, and no matter how much he does to change things, whether this be earning more money or receiving a knighthood, he will never fully be part of this world. Whereas Gerald, because of his parents, is naturally part of the world Birling longs to be a part of.

There is something a little humiliating about how Birling confides in Gerald that 'I might find my way into the next Honours list - just a knighthood, of course'. Birling is desperate to join Gerald's world, and Gerald knows it. One of the reasons he is so relaxed around Birling is because he knows he is Birling's social superior, even though he is younger.

Gerald understands the game Birling is playing. By telling Gerald, Birling wants the news to get back to Sir George and Lady Croft. Gerald makes that easy for Birling by saying 'could I say something to my mother about this? I know she'd be delighted.' Birling of course is happy for this to happen.

When Eric arrives it is clear that Gerald sees himself much more on the side of Birling than Eric, even though the two young men would be about the same age. When there is a knock on the door and it is announced that an Inspector Goole has called, Gerald says 'lightly': 'Eric's probably been up to something (*Nodding confidentially to Birling*)'. He implies that he and Birling had been talking about Eric before Eric came in. This is rather an unpleasant thing to do, and quite bullying. Again, demonstrating to us that he is very much like Birling in his attitude towards those who are less powerful than him.

THE INSPECTOR ARRIVES

Like the others, Gerald cannot work the Inspector out when he arrives. He is sure he won't be needed, saying to Birling 'would't you rather I was out of this?' He believes that this is only to do with Birling's family.

As we have seen time and again, when Birling tries to show off, telling the Inspector who Gerald is ('son of George Croft'), the Inspector is not even slightly impressed. This puts Gerald in a difficult position, as he is used to having the upper hand because of his social status. Without this he's a bit of a fish out of water.

Throughout Birling's interrogation, Gerald is very much on Birling's side. When Birling admits that Eva 'had to go' because of her attempted strike, Gerald says 'You really couldn't have done anything else.' This is in contrast to Eric, who says that he could have kept Eva on. Gerald still wants to keep in Birling's good books, and enjoys the closeness he has with the man.

Why is this? Is it because he is in love with Sheila? Obviously he feels a good deal of affection for her, but as we're soon to find out he was having a relationship with Daisy/Eva whilst seeing Sheila. So not exactly Mr Right. We now also know that his mother disproves of him wanting to marry a socially inferior girl. No, it is more likely that he wants to ingratiate himself with Birling and get on the inside of the family so that he can further his own business interests.

Now I'm sure there is some affection there, don't get me wrong. I'm not totally cynical about this. But let's face it, now we know what sort of world Gerald is a part of, we cannot believe that his intentions are only because of some Romeo-like selfless affection he has for his Juliet? Yes, I think we can agree on this. Gerald is only really looking out for himself.

As Birling says, Crofts Ltd and Birlings can potentially create a monopoly that would be good for both businesses. And Gerald's marriage to Sheila could be just what both families need.

DURING SHEILA'S INTERROGATION

Notice how similar Gerald is to Birling when Sheila is questioned. He tries to pull rank, saying things like 'I'd like to look at that photograph now, Inspector.' His tone is assertive - he is not asking whether he might see it, but rather that he expects to. When the Inspector refuses, he says 'Getting a bit heavy-handed, aren't you Inspector?'

You can imagine Gerald using this tone with his social inferiors at work. However, unlike his employees, the Inspector will not be intimidated.

There is irony when Gerald says 'we're respectable citizens and not dangerous criminals', particularly when the Inspector replies 'Sometimes there isn't as much difference as you might think.' To Gerald, the fact that they are of high social standing, respected by other families and with a solid position in society, means that they are a million miles away from lower class criminals.

Of course, the Inspector is right - just because a family has wealth, power and privilege, doesn't make them immune from criminal behaviour. It is often the most wealthy and powerful that are the most corrupt, often because think they can get away with it.

And this is exactly why the Inspector is with them: to make them understand that they cannot continue to live this sort of life and expect to get away with it. Sooner or later, this sort of behaviour catches up with people.

Do you notice anything about Gerald throughout the two halves of Sheila's interrogation? No? Nothing at all? That's because he says virtually nothing. At no time does he leap to his fiancee's defence, even when the Inspector says 'It's too late, she's dead.' It is only when the Inspector mentions that Eva changed her name to Daisy Renton that Gerald seems to come back to life.

GERALD CONFESSES TO HIS AFFAIR

As we know, Sheila works out straight away that Gerald had been having an affair with Daisy. OK, some of you may be thinking 'yes, typical man, can't keep that guilty look from his face' and you may be right. Gerald is probably not the most devious of men: whilst knowing he's in a superior position in life, he's still just a young man and not able to hide things from his fiancee.

He begins by trying to appeal to her softer side by saying 'Now, listen darling - ' but Sheila cuts him off. She isn't interested in any of the language he's used to this point - as far as she's concerned, the rules have changed and so should the language.

However, he's a bit naive when he says 'for God's sake - don't say anything to the Inspector!' We've already examined Sheila's response to this, which is something like: *don't be a muppet, Gerry, the Inspector knows EVERYTHING ALREADY* (that's me paraphrasing for comic effect). But Gerald is still thinking of his reputation, and that of his family.

Remember: when the most important thing in your life is how others see you, anything that might potentially damage this has to be avoided at all costs. Sadly for Gerald, that ain't gonna happen.

You can run, but you can't hide.

ACT 2: THE INSPECTOR QUESTIONS GERALD

Remember what we said about how Gerald treats Sheila at the start of Act 2? He wants her out of the room because he doesn't want her hearing all the sordid details, so uses the excuse that she's probably a bit hysterical.

We are beginning to realise that everything Gerald does, even if it seems that he has others' best intentions at heart, is in fact quite selfish. It's just part of the world he lives in. As Birling told him just before the Inspector arrived, it's 'every man for himself'.

He shows his true colours when he says to Sheila that the reason she wants to stay is because 'You've been through it and you want to see someone else go through it.' What a thing to say! It really doesn't say much about how Gerald sees Sheila.

As far as he is concerned, the only reason Sheila could possibly want to stay there is to see Gerald uncomfortable. But of course for Sheila it's not that at all: she already realises that the truth is the only thing that matters, and she wants to hear the truth no matter what.

As his questioning continues, so Gerald begins to see what is happening, and how his behaviour has resulted in the death of an innocent young girl. He admits to meeting her at the Palace bar and 'rescuing' her from 'Old Joe Meggarty', who was drunkenly trying to seduce her. Gerald took her from the place to another bar and they talked. She told him how hard things were for her, and that she was hungry.

What she was doing was playing to his instinctive need to protect. I'm not saying that as a negative thing, as perhaps anyone in that situation would have done the same thing. But she could probably see a wealthy, unmarried young man who had taken an interest in her, and she wasn't going to let that go. Was she being manipulative? Impossible to say. More likely she was simply desperate and grateful that Gerald had rescued her from a drunken old man.

Now, Gerald tells the Inspector (but actually more to Sheila) that he didn't 'install' Daisy in his friends place 'to make love to her'. And perhaps he is telling the truth. But his instinct to protect turned into something more. A need somehow to possess Daisy, to take pleasure from her.

Remember: Gerald is the sort of man who is used to getting his own way. So when a pretty young girl shows gratitude to him, sees him as a sort of hero, these protective feelings became something more selfish.

Sheila makes it clear - 'You were the wonderful Fairy Prince. You must have adored it, Gerald.' He won't lie about that: of course he did. At this point in the play he is being honest and Sheila can see that. It is about the only time that he truly opens up, and for a moment we can see a vulnerability that his previous confidence was masking.

It's interesting that Gerald actually finds it hard that Daisy did not blame him for ending their relationship: 'She didn't blame me at all. I wish to God she had now. Perhaps I'd feel better about it.'

Why is this? Why on earth would he feel better about what happened to her if she had been angry or aggressive, had blamed him for ruining her life? Because the relationship ended with Daisy being the better person, the more mature, noble one. And so there is no way he can feel negative towards her because, even at the end, she was good. (We'll shortly analyse Eva/Daisy and see how important her character is, even though we never meet her.)

Before he leaves, he tells Sheila he understands why she has given back the engagement ring, and why they 'aren't the same people who sat down to dinner'. We feel a little warmer towards Gerald at this point: he has admitted to his role in Eva/Daisy's death, apologised for the hurt he has caused, and understood that things are very different now and that he has to change.

But, as we will see later, when he leaves the Birlings' house it isn't just to walk around and calm down. He has his own detective work to do...

GERALD IN ACT 3

Gerald reappears after the Inspector has left. He immediately changes the tone of the room by confidently declaring 'That man wasn't a police officer.' He tells them that he had met a police sergeant he knows, and that this man had confirmed that no Inspector Goole worked at the station. Of course Birling is over the moon, excitedly saying 'Good lad' to Gerald.

Gerald concludes 'There isn't any such inspector. We've been *had*.' From this point, nothing Sheila or Eric can say will make Birling or his wife feel anything other than huge relief. This relief intensifies when Gerald, acting like a police inspector himself, questions first of all whether it was only one girl, and then whether there was anyone dead in the infirmary at all.

He is clearly enjoying being the centre of attention at this point, as 'He looks around triumphantly at them' when he explains that none of them could know it was the same person as the Inspector could have showed them all different girls.

Birling becomes more and more animated as Gerald further concludes that there might not even be a dead girl, which of course he confirms when he calls the hospital. He is utterly deaf to what

Sheila is saying over and over, only interested in the fact that he has solved the riddle and proven that there is nothing to worry about.

The very last thing he says, before they discover that there is indeed a dead girl at the infirmary, is 'Everything's all right now... What about this ring?' As far as he is concerned, the only thing that was keeping them apart was the impending scandal that the Inspector had uncovered. Now that he has proven the whole thing was a hoax, he cannot see why things can't go back the way they were before.

What he fails to see, which shows how little he has actually changed, is how it is not the truth or otherwise of the girl's death, but rather the fact that he'd had an affair. He seems to believe that it isn't such a big deal: why else would he assume Sheila will accept the ring back?

This shows us how deeply rooted his sense of entitlement is. Of course she'll accept him back - why shouldn't she? We know why: he has shown his true colours, and Sheila's not sure they're the right ones for her.

INSPECTOR GOOLE

The Inspector is the catalyst, the reason the characters are made to confront their prejudices and learn (or not learn) how to be better people as a result. As we mentioned earlier, his name is a bit ghost-like (Goole/ghoul) and we can question how real he actually was.

But what is more important than who he is is what he does, and what he represents. Remember: characters aren't real people. They are vehicles through which the writer explores the world.

THE INSPECTOR'S ENTRANCE

Look carefully at the precise moment the Inspector enters. Birling has just lectured Eric and Gerald on the importance of looking after numero uno, and ended by saying 'I wanted you to have the benefit of my experience'.

It is no coincidence that Goole enters at this point, as his whole purpose is to show this so-called 'experience' for what it really is: a load of ignorant hot air.

The stage directions describe Goole as someone who 'creates an impression of massiveness, solidity, and purposefulness…and has a disconcerting habit of looking hard at the person he addresses before actually speaking'. It will be as much about how he acts with these people as what he actually says. This 'looking hard' is important: it is as if he is able to look into each character's hearts and see them for who they really are.

He is initially polite with Birling, addressing him as 'sir' and then 'Mr Birling'. It is only later that this politeness disappears as he becomes more short tempered and frustrated at the responses he receives.

At this point he has no need to be more aggressive as he does not yet know the responses he will receive. This is because his whole approach rests on mirroring back to each character their response to him. If they cooperate he is easier on them (Sheila); if they continue to maintain an arrogant belief they're right, he will become more and more direct and pointed (Mrs Birling).

Birling first dismisses the reason the Inspector says he is there: 'Yes yes. Horrible business…But I don't understand why you should come here, Inspector-?' Goole cuts through 'massively': he is not prepared to allow anyone to question his purpose for being there. He has a line of enquiry and will not be deterred.

What we see Goole able to do from very early on is lead each character into saying exactly what he wants him to say. Take Gerald for example. Goole seems to be interested in the fact that this is 'Mr Gerald Croft' who is going to marry 'Miss Sheila Birling'. Gerald says '(Smiling) I hope so.' To which the Inspector replies '(Gravely) Then I'd prefer you to stay'.

They were thinking that Goole was impressed that he was speaking to these important people, when in fact he was mocking them. He couldn't care less who they were: he wants the truth, no more no less, whoever they think they are.

Goole makes it very clear to them all why he is here. It is all about the 'chain of events' that led to Eva/Daisy's suicide, that started with Birling firing her from her job. We will see that this is less about interrogating individuals and more about telling a story, one that every person in that house is involved in, for better or worse.

What makes us realise that this man is not your average police inspector is when he begins to comment on some of the things characters admit to. When Birling says 'If you don't come down sharply on some of these people, they'd soon be asking the earth', Goole replies '..after all it's better to ask the earth than to take it.'

What does he mean by this? He is referring of course to human greed, to men like Birling who are happy to exploit the earth and its resources for their own material gain. What Priestley is suggesting is that what it all boils down to is greed: why there are wars, why people ruin other people's lives, why all the terrible things happen in the world. Because one man wants more of the earth and is prepared to trample on people in order to get it.

QUESTIONING SHEILA

This approach continues when Sheila enters. He tells her that 'There are a lot of young women living that sort of existence, Miss Birling, in every city and big town in this country. It it weren't, the factories and warehouses wouldn't know where to look for cheap labour. Ask your father.'

This is the opposite view to Birling. As far as Birling is concerned, it is a free market and employees can go where they choose. If they don't like the conditions of one place of work they are free to work somewhere else. But for Goole, it's not that simple. The reason wages are so low is because there are plenty of people desperate for work who will accept low wages and poor conditions.

The time at which the play is set, as well as when it was written, are important to consider when it comes to workers' rights. The Welfare State was first launched in Britain at the time the play was set: the Liberal party were in power, and moved ahead with a series of reforms including a minimum wage in 1909 for certain low wage industries, free school meals in 1906, and pensions in 1908.

However, much of these reforms weren't fully implemented until the 1940s, with the National Health Service introduced in 1946 after being proposed in 1944. So Priestley was writing at a time of great change in society, which was moving away from a capitalist, free market economy towards one that emphasised the importance of looking after the less fortunate.

What we can therefore say is that Inspector Goole very much represents the reforming voice, the one that demanded change in society, and Birling represents the old, capitalist way of looking at the world.

Goole continues to reflect characters' words back on them. When Birling says 'We were having a nice family celebration tonight. And a nasty mess you've made of it now, haven't you?' Goole replies 'That's more or less what I was thinking earlier tonight....A nice promising life there...and a nasty mess somebody's made of it'.

He even admits to his approach by saying to Gerald 'If you're easy with me, I'm easy with you'. It is entirely up to each character how the Inspector behaves towards them: if they work out these new rules the interrogation will be less fierce. If they don't, they'll incur his wrath.

GOOLE THE THERAPIST

One way of looking at Goole is to imagine him more like a therapist than a police officer. If you look at how he responds to Sheila when she admits what she did, you'll see what I mean. He begins by taking what Sheila tells him and drawing a conclusion: 'In fact, in a kind of way, you might be said to be jealous of her?'

Look first of all at how he says this. He is not being aggressive or confrontational - if anything, he is being quite gentle on Sheila. This is because she has fully opened up and has already admitted to her wrongdoing. She is ashamed and so there is no reason for Goole to twist the knife. Instead, what he does is to help articulate what she is feeling.

He continues by saying 'And so you used the power you had, as a daughter of a good customer…to punish the girl just because she made you feel like that.' This is the cold, hard truth, and of course it hurts Sheila. But it's supposed to. That's the whole point! None of them can heal until their wounds are opened up and allowed to breathe.

It is only when Sheila uses the old 'if only I knew then what I know now' technique that the Inspector changes his tone, saying harshly 'It's too late. She's dead.' We'll see this rather unorthodox approach used throughout his questioning: he will stop at times and make comment on what he hears, bringing a personal response into the interrogations that is highly unusual for a police inspector and does get the slightly more astute characters (aka Sheila) to begin to question who this man actually is.

QUESTIONING GERALD

What you may notice, as I write this analysis of Goole's character, is that I spend less time on the actual questioning and more on the things he says in between. There's a good reason for this: when he questions, the play moves along as one might expect any crime interrogation to move. I don't think we learn a huge amount about the Inspector himself through this questioning. The other characters yes, but not Goole.

It is when he pauses and comments on how the characters act and react, and makes comment on the life of Eva/Daisy, that we learn the most about him. Take what he says to Gerald about why he thinks it better Sheila stays and hears the detail about Gerald's affair: 'Miss Birling has just been made to understand what she did to this girl. She feels responsible. And if she leaves now, and doesn't hear any more, then she'll feel she's entirely to blame, she'll be alone with her responsibility…You see, we have to share something. If there's nothing else, we have to share our guilt.'

As we've explored a little before, this is a profoundly important quote. What does he mean, 'If there's nothing else'? I think what he means is this: perhaps we cannot share wealth, or status, or anything that separates us from others.

But what we have to share is a collective guilt at what happens in the world. That war and famine and disease are not isolated things that happen to people other than us, but things that happen because of us. Take global warming: every one of us has a part to play in that.

We have to take responsibility for the world and the people in it. For it is people like the Birlings that have caused all the grief in the world and have taken none of the responsibility.

So, Gerald's questioning takes a fairly standard turn, with Goole urging Gerald to give more and more detail until he has said everything he can and Sheila ends by saying 'I don't dislike you half as much as I did half an hour ago.'

It would appear that Goole has been successful with Gerald, opening him up and giving him the opportunity to apologise for what he did.

QUESTIONING MRS BIRLING

Mrs Birling's attitude towards Goole is very different from the others. She is defensive and haughty, and we can see starts to wind the Inspector up. When Mrs Birling says 'and what business it is of yours?', Goole 'severely' says 'Do you want me to tell you - in plain words?' He will not be bullied by these people - he has a job to do and he plans to do it.

Goole has no trouble in getting Mrs Birling to admit that she was prejudiced against Eva's case because she found her impudent, and that it was her influence that had the girl's case thrown out.

However, Mrs Birling will not back down and admit she was wrong, so Goole changes his approach a little: 'I think you did something terribly wrong - and that you're going to spend the rest of your life regretting it. I wish you'd been with me tonight at the infimary...'

He then informs them all that Eva was going to have a baby. And, as we have seen before, he attempts to draw on Mrs Birling's emotions by saying 'She came to you for help, at a time when no woman could have needed it more...And you slammed the door in her face.'

Finally, Mrs Birling becomes 'agitated'! It took Goole appealing to her feminine side, the nurturing part of Mrs Birling that surely must be buried there somewhere. However, she soon regains her composure but the Inspector doesn't let up. He continues to press her with questions, trying to break her down and admit she was wrong. But she does not.

Instead, what she does of course is pile all the blame onto Eric, only without realising it. Goole makes her admit that the fault ultimately lies with the young man who got Eva pregnant, but Mrs Birling is either too blinkered or too ignorant to realise who he is referring to.

Goole's technique, as we have seen with each character so far, is to take the ugliest parts of their personalities and magnify them. With Birling it was his greed, with Sheila her vanity, with Gerald his desperate need to be a hero and be adored, and with Mrs Birling her arrogant pride.

What is interesting is that it has been Mrs Birling who has been the hardest person to break through: in fact, it is only when she realises that it is Eric the Inspector is referring to that she seems broken. Why is this? Probably because the pride that comes from her upper class status is the most ingrained into her.

Unlike Sheila, who quickly sees that her jealousy of Eva's beauty caused her to lash out and act appallingly, Mrs Birling's superior status is part of her life, so she cannot simply step outside of it and see it for what it is.

It's an interesting comment on just how ingrained social status was at the time the play was set.

ERIC IN ACT 3

We don't need to spend too long on Goole's questioning of Eric as we've just seen how he freely and openly admits to his wrongdoing and seems ashamed at the person he has become.

What is interesting is how much more urgent Goole is at this point. On several occasions he wants to hurry the questioning on, saying things like 'Don't start on that. I want to get on' and 'I don't want any of that from you. Settle it afterwards.'

Perhaps he knows that very soon the police station will call and announce that a girl has actually died? It's hard to stay - but what is clear is that Goole wants to get to the end of this questioning and leave so that they have time to discuss the implications before the station calls for real. Or perhaps he simply bored of them and their pathetic internal squabbles and wants the whole truth out. We certainly see them for the fractured family they actually are at this point.

As the Inspector concludes his interrogation of the characters, what we notice is just how far he has broken them apart. They began the evening as one unit, celebrating an important stage in their daughter's (and Birling hopes his business's) development, and have ended it at war with one another, with two children who now profoundly distrust their parents and parents who simply no longer know their children.

What Priestley seems to be saying here is this: the basis of this so-called stable society is the 'nuclear family': parents and children living in harmony with one another, with a powerful patriarch at the top of the family supported by his obedient wife and children.

If it is men like Birling and women like Mrs Birling who represent those in power, then no wonder society is in such a mess. These lives built on lies and the oppression of the weak can only end badly. At least it's certainly ended badly for this lot.

His concluding remarks are brutal. After he has commanded them to 'Stop!', for fear that they will begin to physically attack one another, he forcefully reminds them that 'each of you helped kill her. Remember that. Never forget it.'

He then gives a bleak summary of the role each character played in her death: Mrs Birling who 'refused her the pitiable little bit of organised charity you had in your power to grant her'. Eric who 'used her for the end of a stupid drunken evening as if she was an animal, a thing, not a person. And Birling, who 'wanted twenty five shillings a week instead of twenty-two. You made her pay a heavy price for that. And now she'll make you pay a heavier price still.'

It is almost biblical, isn't it? As if the Inspector is some avenging angel, come down to seek justice. An eye for an eye, if you like.

And this is the whole point. Priestley isn't trying to create some realistic drama here - he wants there to be a mysterious, mystical element to the whole thing. Goole is a bit like the Ghost of Christmas Past in 'A Christmas Carol', who has come to haunt the family and try to make them change their ways, just as the Ghosts did to Scrooge. This man has arrived to tell them that there will be repercussions to their actions, sooner or later.

And of course we know that is true when they discover that a girl really has died.

That final speech he gives, which we looked at briefly during the Act by Act summary, is worth turning to again, as it really does sum up the entire point Priestley wrote the play. Remember what Goole says:

'One Eva Smith has gone - but there are millions and millions of Eva Smiths and John Smiths still left with us, with their lives, their hopes and fears, their suffering and chance of happiness, all intertwined with our lives, with what we think and say and do. We don't live alone. We are members of one body. We are responsible for each other. And I tell you that the time will soon come when if men will not learn that lesson, then they will be taught it in fire and blood and anguish.'

Powerful words! And again, that last point he makes really does sound biblical. Of course he's right - the two World Wars will soon follow, which is about as much fire, blood and anguish as the world has ever seen, or is ever likely to see. Remember: Priestley is writing through the lens of the mid 1940s, at the end of the Second World War. He has fought in one and suffered through another and he doesn't want it to happen again.

This is what makes the play so powerful, and the reason it remains popular today. Yes, it is set in 1912, but its themes are relevant today. If we continue to treat others as less than ourselves, if we act in a way which is motivated by greed, then we will bring great suffering on the world. Our individual actions may not seem to be much more than a tiny ripple in a pool, but because our lives are 'inter-twined' every action can have massive consequences later, just as happened with Eva Smith.

When the Inspector leaves, it is not only the characters who are left to ponder his profoundly important words. It is the audience, made up I'm sure of men and women just like the Birlings. I wonder whether it made a difference to how they thought? The changes in society that took place from the mid 1940s onwards would suggest that yes, plays like this were part of the narrative that defined Britain and much of Europe in the years to come.

EVA SMITH / DAISY RENTON

Even though we never meet her, it's worth spending a few minutes looking at how Priestley represents Eva/Daisy and the role she has in the play.

From the very start of the play, the Inspector presents her as a pitiable figure who is only trying to make her way in the world, but who is continually pushed down and abused by the members of the Birling family.

The first hint we get that Eva is more than just another girl who'd experienced bad luck is when Goole says 'This young woman, Eva Smith, was a bit out of the ordinary'. Even from the beginning we get the impression that she was a bit of a fish out of water, perhaps in the wrong life, without the toughness to survive.

The other way we could read this is that Goole is hinting that Eva/Daisy is not an ordinary person, ie. she is part of the mysticism that surrounds Goole and his approach. Like Goole, she is somehow a ghost, a vehicle used to explore the Birling family's prejudices.

EVA'S APPEARANCE

We notice how often her looks are referred to. Birling mentions that she was a 'lively, good looking girl', Sheila calls her a 'very pretty girl... with soft fine hair and grey eyes', Gerald calls her 'very pretty - soft brown hair and big dark eyes', and Eric says she was 'pretty and a good sport'.

Each of these tell us a little about the characters: Birling (sort of) makes her sound like a horse, Sheila and Gerald both pick out the quality of her hair and her eyes (which Gerald makes sound quite seductive), and Eric refers to her being good fun.

What is clear is that each of them had a reaction to her looks, and that this varied from appreciation (Birling) to jealousy (Sheila) to attraction (Gerald) to lust (Eric). With three of them, this frames what happens next: Sheila has Eva sacked, Gerald begins by helping her and then has an affair, and Eric has a drunken night with her that turns into something more.

It is not often you'd say that someone's looks were a curse, but in this case you probably can. Eva almost certainly wouldn't have ended up dead unless she'd been good looking.

Goole uses her looks to hammer home the ugliness of her death. When Sheila arrives during Birling's interrogation and asks if Eva had been pretty, Goole replies 'She wasn't pretty when I saw her today, but she had been pretty - very pretty.'

Her looks are an important tool for the Inspector: by highlighting how her suicide has destroyed her looks he can appeal to a girl like Sheila who knows how important looks are to a girl.

EVA'S PATHETIC LIFE

Goole continually highlights how pathetic Eva's life was, and how she is representative of countless others just like her. When questioning Sheila, he suggests that 'it would do us all a bit of good if sometimes we tried to put ourselves in the place of these young women counting their pennies in their dingy little back bedrooms'.

Those small details tell us a huge amount about how Priestley wants us to imagine girls like Eva. Alone, poor, surrounded by their pathetic lives, just surviving day to day. It is a powerful image, made all the more haunting by what we know happened to her.

One of the things that most separates Goole's approach to the more traditional approach to questioning is how he paints a picture of Eva/Daisy's life in the time leading up to her meeting each member of the family.

Take a look at the introduction to Sheila meeting her:

"And it happened that at the beginning of December that year - 1910 - there was a good deal of influenza about, and Milwards suddenly found themselves short-handed. So that gave her her chance. And from what I can gather, she liked working there. It was a nice change from the factory. She enjoyed being among pretty clothes, I've no doubt. And now she felt she was making a good fresh start. You can imagine how she felt."

It's probably pretty obvious why Goole does this. It isn't so that any of those being questioned have a greater understanding of the girl. It is to make them feel guilty, pure and simple.

Just look at the language he uses: *she had a chance, it was a nice change, she was making a good fresh start, you can imagine…* All of this is to place a privileged woman like Sheila into Eva's shoes, so that she can understand how devastating it was to lose that job.

This is Goole's main purpose: he wants them to realise that this woman had a life leading up to their meeting with her, and that her descent towards suicide was a gradual process. That they met her at just one stage in her life and helped her on her way to suicide.

This is a powerful message, and one that Priestley is trying to communicate in stark terms to his audience. Our lives are on a continuum - a line from birth to death. None of us can escape that. But we often forget that its the same for others.

How often do we get angry with someone who is rude to us, or upset when people don't do what we'd like them to do? We often forget that we meet these people at one point in their lives, and we have no idea what came before.

Priestley is reminding us that even the smallest action can have consequences further along the line. I guess he's trying to make us more thoughtful people, more aware of how others feel. Not a bad goal, really.

EVA AS A MAGNIFYING GLASS

As we've mentioned before, Eva/Daisy brings out the fundamental nature of each of the characters she interacts with. It's as if she knows exactly which buttons to push in order to reveal how ugly each of these people are. She acts as a magnifying glass, enlarging the family's faults so they can more clearly be interrogated by the Inspector.

With Birling, it's his greed. He doesn't want Eva or any of her colleagues to earn more, as it will take away some of his profits.

For Sheila, it is all about Eva's looks in relation to hers. Eva is prettier and that's enough to make Sheila act in the way she does. Sheila is insecure and jealous, and takes it out on Eva.

For Gerald, it's the fact that Eva/Daisy is the 'damsel in distress': he is attracted to her as a vulnerable woman who is desperately in need of help. Gerald is a vain man who clearly likes female attention as it makes him feel better about himself.

For Eric, it is nothing more than lust: he is governed by the carnal/sexual need to have Eva, no matter what the cost. However, he is also driven by shame, and steals money to help Eva when he discovers she is pregnant.

For Mrs Birling, it is sheer arrogant pride that stops her from helping Eva. She cannot bear the fact that Eva calls herself Mrs Birling, even though we know she does this because of her former relationship with Eric and not because she is being disrespectful.

We've mentioned before this idea of Eva being a vehicle through which the Inspector is able to pull apart the family's prejudices. This is why it is actually unimportant whether there is more than one Eva, or whether a dead girl existed at all. Sheila and Eric get this by the end: Eva/Daisy is a tool and nothing more.

As I've said before, think of her like a surgeon's scalpel, used to slice each character open and pull out all the bad stuff. Whether each character is sliced open by a different scalpel is irrelevant. Each has their own sharp blade which reveals the dark side of their character.

3

THE THEMES

INTRODUCTION TO THEMES

So, we've spent a fair bit of time on character, so you should be getting a pretty good feel for how Priestley uses each of them to explore these big themes.

We don't need to spend too long on the themes, but it's probably worth summarising each of them so we can see the bigger picture.

WHAT IS A THEME?

Glad you asked me that. Us teachers are always banging on about them, but rarely take the time to explain what they are.

A theme is an idea that recurs throughout a book, play or poem. If you like, it's the writer wanting to explore something that is important to them, an idea about the world, maybe a concern they have or something they are passionate about.

Themes are important as they act as the glue that sticks a play like this together. Without them, this play would be all about a family having a nice meal in a room and congratulating themselves on how clever they all are. Without them, there would be no Inspector calling.

Themes can usually be summarised in a sentence or two. If we think about this play, some of the themes are:

•*Social Class*. The class you are born into is something you can never leave, that determines the amount of power and control you have over others.

•*Capitalism and the fear of Socialism*. In a capitalist society, you look after number one no matter the cost to those with less power than you. Socialists are not to be trusted as they seek to undermine a system that works in favour of those in power.

•*The importance of the nuclear family*. A stable society begins with a stable home. Anything that disrupts this family stability can have consequences in society as a whole. How men are seen by women, and how women act around men, is an important part of this.

•*Responsibility and blame*. We are all responsible for how we treat others, but many seek to pass the blame to others when they do not wish to confront their own failings.

Let's look at each of these in turn and see where they show their ugly faces.

SOCIAL CLASS

As we've discussed a few times, social class is one of the biggest and most important themes of the play. In fact, you could call it the 'uber-theme', as all the others sit underneath it.

What you need to understand about the time the play was written is that social class was a lot more important than it is today. Nowadays we don't talk about it as much - we live in a more meritocratic society - in other words, we are able to move up the career ladder because of merit, or how hard we work, and not because of who our daddy is and where we went to school.

Of course, there are always exceptions (just look at the Conservative party and how many old Etonians there are) but you'll often find people from a working class background who've become multi millionnaire entrepreneurs. And with the growth of computing and the internet that's even easier than before.

In 1912, the vision between upper, middle and lower classes was firm and fixed. You were upper class if you came from 'old money' - you inherited your wealth from your parents. You were middle class if you had made your own money. And you were lower/working class if you only had enough money to get by on day to day - and often not even that.

The lower classes are there to be exploited by people like Birling. As far as he is concerned they are expendable. There is a name for this attitude to working classes: seeing these 'lesser people' as *canon-fodder*. This comes from warfare: thousands of men being mown down and killed by canons on the battle field, with each individual life having little value, as there are always more men following on behind. We see this at its most terrible in the trenches of the First World War.

MR BIRLING - THE SELF-MADE MAN

The theme of class is perfectly shown in the character of Mr Birling. Birling is a man who has built a large and successful business, but did not originally come from money. We can tell this because of his accent - Priestley refers to it as 'provincial' - and how he asks Sybil to thank cook for the meal. He betrays his working class origins through these little giveaways, but is desperate to move properly into the upper classes.

He admires men like Sir George Croft, largely because he has a knighthood, which is what Birling craves. Birling sees a knighthood as his ticket into the higher echelons of society, and he is prepared to do whatever it takes to get it.

We know this because of how he treats his family throughout the Inspector's visit. He is quite prepared to throw his two children under the bus in order to deflect as much of the blame away from himself as possible. However, very little blame is thrown either Gerald's or Mrs Birling's way, largely because of their upper class background.

Class is everything to a man like Birling, because the higher he moves the more power and influence he will have. To Priestley, he represents everything that is wrong with capitalism: he is selfish, power-hungry and arrogant.

MRS BIRLING - UPPER CLASS AND SHE KNOWS IT

Remember what we said before about how your social class is fixed? This is why women like Mrs Birling aren't worried about suddenly losing their position in society, because as someone who was born into money she has a security that Birling does not have.

What Mrs Birling is most worried about is ensuring that those around her stick to the rules. If you look at how she acts throughout most of the play, she is continually trying to maintain a strict set of protocols (rules for living).

They include things like respecting your parents, being spoken to respectfully by those of a lower class or status, and not talking about unpleasant things. This seems to be her main role in the family, as a sort of 'etiquette police'. However, as the Inspector probes deeper and deeper so Mrs Birling's influence fades away, and she finds she has less and less control over what her family says.

What does this tell us about class? That it is just a veneer, an outward set of appearances and rules, and does not give us the truth about who someone really is. Because when you look at it, it's the character with the highest social standing who acts in the most appalling way, whereas both the Inspector and Eva/Daisy come out of it all looking pretty good. Apart from the disinfectant of course.

Mrs Birling is so caught up in her own self importance that she has lost her essential humanity. Quite sad when you think of it.

EVA SMITH - A WORKING CLASS ICON

Look back at how the Inspector presents Eva/Daisy. It is quite idealised. The struggling young girl, desperate to make her way in the world, fighting for a decent wage, grateful for a second chance, pushed from one man to the next before the ultimate slap in the face from the one woman who could have saved her when she was at her most vulnerable and alone.

Remind you of anyone? Possibly not. But the arc/journey of her character is a little Christlike, don't you think? Born into nothing, fighting for the rights of the less fortunate, but ultimately betrayed by those in power.

Priestley doesn't do this by accident. He wants the audience to feel a deep compassion for this woman. She is not a doormat - like Jesus, she was prepared to stand up for what she believed in. But life conspired to deal her a poor hand of cards, and that last act of self-sacrifice is the tragic end to a life that could have been so much better, were others to have treated her with more respect and compassion.

You see, Eva represents every working class woman or man who has been unfairly treated by society because of the sheer misfortune of being born into nothing. When you think of it, it is just luck: we don't choose who are parents are, and some are born into a world of opportunity they have done nothing to deserve.

She could have been a different woman to every single member of the family and it really wouldn't matter, as each one of them abused their position in society by abusing her.

The Inspector's final comments, just before he leaves, are the most important in this regard. That there are thousands just like Eva, and they all want to make their lives better, and it is up to all of us to work together to make this a reality.

Is it idealistic? Of course it is. But remember when this play was written: the war had just ended and people were filled with a hope that the world had learned its lessons and a new society could be built. In some ways we have seen big improvements, such as the NHS, but in other ways I'm sure Priestley would be disappointed at the high levels of poverty still in evidence across the world.

THE FAMILY

We've looked at this a few times already, but it's worth mentioning again what the family represents in society.

A strong, stable family unit sits at the centre of modern society. Why do you think marriage was invented? It wasn't in order to enable couples to formally show the world how much they love each other. I'm afraid not. Marriage is a contract, legally binding, between two people.

And back at the time the play was written, this was even more the case. Of course, love might come into it, but not always. Traditionally, upper and middle class marriages were seen as a way of furthering the interests of the two families who would be joined together.

This is certainly the case with the impending marriage of Sheila and Gerald. Birling can see how having Gerald close to the family won't hurt his chances with his competitor - he is more interested in this than any emotional reasons why Sheila might wish to marry Gerald.

So, the play begins with the family celebrating this engagement. Other than Eric, who even at the start of the play seems a little separate from the others, they give off a sense of being very much together, laughing and joking, all within the strict parameters Mrs Birling has set.

It is only when the Inspector arrives, and begins to tear apart each family member, that we can see cracks occuring in the family's unity. Mr and Mrs Birling begin to focus on themselves, even at the cost of their children, such is their desire to maintain their good name.

However, they know how important it is to ensure the world sees them as a respectable family unit, so when this is called into question they respond aggressively. Birling will know that his chances of a knighthood will be all but destroyed if it gets out that his son got a poor woman pregnant then stole from the family business to pay her off. Family life and public life are intertwined: a good public servant should have an impeccable private life.

All this is totally hypocritical: both Sheila and Eric mention some of their father's colleagues, who are drunks and womanisers, all the while seemingly upstanding family men. But this is different from your son being out of control: it will be expected that important men like Birling will take a mistress, and their wives can do little about it - we know this because of Mrs Birling's advice to her daughter at the start of the play.

However, if you can't control your children, and they start stealing from you, people will begin to question your role in society. This is why Birling suddenly changes his tune with the Inspector in Act 1 when he realises that this is not all about him. He is worried because he has no idea what any of his family have done so he can't control the message.

Think of the Birlings as a **microcosm** of society as a whole. Microcosm literally means 'small world'. That the small world of this family represents the broader world: the stability of the family unit representing the wider stability of society.

We hear a lot about the number of divorces and single parent families, and some newspapers get quite animated about how this will lead to society collapsing. You see, it's as relevant a worry today as it was one hundred years ago: a lot of people are scared that, without a stable home to grow up in, kids will become criminal etc.

It's all a big generalisation as there are so many factors that determine how people grow up, but it's worth bearing in mind that the ideal of the 'nuclear family' is as much a concern of today's society as it was in 1912.

CAPITALISM AND SOCIALISM

We've already talked about how Birling represents the typical capitalist. Capitalism is an economic system based on privately owned companies and making profit. A capitalist society will offer incentives to men like Birling in order for them to build profitable businesses and employ more and more people. It's been the major form of world economics for around 200 years, and won't be leaving us any time soon.

One supposed advantage of capitalism is that it is supposed to motivate people to make the most of their lives. If you can be a 'self made man', building a big business, then you deserve the rewards. The disadvantages are seen in the play: in order to build this business you have to make choices, and some of these choices can be bad for other people. Like sacking Eva Smith because she wanted more money.

Broadly speaking (as things are always more subtle than it would appear on the surface), the opposite of capitalism is socialism. Socialists believe in shared wealth: that we should all work for the good of society, not only ourselves. We've seen this in Communist societies like the Soviet Union and China: we still see it in North Korea and (nowadays to a lesser extent) Cuba.

The main advantage of a socialist society (in theory) is that you are looked after by the state no matter your position in society. If you are sick, or old, you will still be looked after by the government. You will have free health care and a job for life if you're able to work. You might be paid in vouchers that you can exchange for food or other services. Everyone should get the same treatment, no matter your position.

Sadly, history has taught us that socialist governments have not always ended well. The Soviet Union and North Korea have been accused of terrible crimes against their people, and many question China's record of human rights abuses.

Why? Good question. You'd have thought that those in charge of these more 'caring' societies would have the best interests of their people at heart. It would appear not. In order to ensure workers are willing to work long hours for little or no pay, many control mechanisms are brought into place, such as terrible prisons for anyone who even look like they might disagree (look up the Soviet Gulags for more detail on this).

And what does any of this have to do with the play? Another good question! (You're full of them today, aren't you.) Priestley is deeply critical of capitalism. He has seen how the selfish actions of those in positions of wealth and power have abused those beneath them (whether this be through businesses like Birling's or the horrors of the two World Wars).

We know that men like Birling are worried about the rise of socialism. He mentions it on more than occasion, calling those who believe in this economic approach 'cranks' (crazy people). Remember that at the time the play was set, Russia was gaining power across the east of Europe, and many were concerned that they might move further west, bringing these socialist ideas into capitalist societies such as Britain. It would be a few more years before the Russian royal family was brutally murdered by the Bolsheviks (the Russian political party who believed in socialism), but the seeds were already being sown.

In 1945, when the play was written, we hadn't seen the ugly truth of Stalin's Soviet Union, with its labour camps and mass starvation. Priestley can see hope in a more caring society, and wants to explore this through the play.

The Inspector very much represents this emerging socialism, which is why he is so distrusted by women like Mrs Birling, who is frankly disgusted by Goole's ideas and approach. He represents to her one of the 'little people', but it is his growing power within the family that Priestley most wants us to witness. By the end he commands centre stage, and no one will question him.

RESPONSIBILITY AND BLAME

The Inspector's primary goal is to make the Birlings take responsibility for their actions and understand that people like them need to change if society is to evolve. When we talk about capitalism, we have also to understand that it can make people quite selfish: if you can make lots of money, you might be inclined to step over people in order to become more successful than them.

I don't want to sound too pessimistic about human nature, but I think we all have a tendency to want to improve our own lives, and this can often mean looking the other way when what we do may not have the best consequences for others.

I don't mean to say that we are all monsters who will do whatever it takes for money and power, but all of us are guilty at times of privileging ourselves over others. But what the Inspector wants the family to do is understand that this way of living can have a devastating effect on others if allowed to accumulate over time.

How well does he do? I think we know the answer to that one. It would seem that the younger the family member, the more effect the Inspector has on them. Sheila and Eric totally get it by the end,

Gerald sort of gets it then goes full circle when he realises Goole was a fake, and the Birling parents don't much change their mind at all.

In fact, Birling is quite prepared to blame everything on Eric by the end. Eric is the weakest link if you like, the one with the least power and influence in the family. Was what he did worse than Birling sacking Eva or Mrs Birling refusing to help her? Of course not: yes, he shouldn't have taken advantage of her, but at least he tried to help her at the end.

The fact is, Birling and his wife take no responsibility for what happened to Eva. And this is why the play ends with a phone call to the police station to tell them all that woman has indeed killed herself swallowing disinfectant, and and Inspector is on his way to question them…

So what does Priestley want us to take away from this play? What lesson does he want us to learn? That's pretty simple: man up and take ownership of your mistakes. Learn from them. Because if you don't, life has a habit of sending you bigger and bigger lessons until you finally realise what you need to learn.

4

TACKLING THE EXAM

In this section I thought I'd delve deeply into the murky old world of the examiner's head (as this is the title of the book series, after all). As you may have seen with my other book (Examiner's Head GCSE English Language - what do you mean you haven't read it?) I think it's useful to work out what the examiner wants you to do in the exam, so you're best prepared to nail the question when you're sitting in the sports hall with a few hundred other sad-looking individuals.

A NOTE ON AOS

No *Examiner's Head* guide would be complete without a little bit of detail on Assessment Objectives. As I mention in my Language GCSE revision guide (more shameless self-promotion) you do need to know about these, as they can make the difference between a grade 4 or 5, or an 8 or 9.

Why do you need to know about them? Because, my friend, if you make sure every single thing you write ticks one of those bad boys, you're on a winner.

Here are the Assessment Objectives for this paper. I've made them student-friendly - aren't I kind?

- **AO1: Read, understand and respond to texts**. This one is all about how closely you read the play, how you use a formal, critical style, and how you bring in your own thoughts. It's also going to mark you on how well you quote.
- **AO2: Language, form and structure.** This one asks you to look carefully at the small details - how the language, form (ie the fact it's a play and not a novel or poem) and structure (how the play is set out) add to the meaning. It also wants you to use the right terminology. We'll come onto that later.
- **AO3: The relationship between texts and the contexts in which they were written.** This one asks you to say something about the historical/social/political context that has somehow shaped the play. You're not going to be writing a history essay, but you are going to mention how the characters and themes of the play are a reflection both on when the play is set (1912) and when it was written (1945).
- **AO4: Write well**. Exactly what it suggests. Use a range of vocabulary, structure your writing well using paragraphs, and watch your spelling.

Interestingly. AO4 is only assessed in Section A (the play section). The other two sections (seen and unseen poetry) aren't assessed for AO4. No idea why. I'd suggest spelling well and using paragraphs throughout as it makes things easier for the examiner.

SAMPLE QUESTIONS

If we look at the AQA questions (as of 2018 there are two papers available - a sample and the 2017 paper), we'll see a pattern emerging:

Sample paper:

How and why does Sheila change in An Inspector Calls? Write about:

how Sheila responds to her family and to the Inspector

how Priestley presents Sheila by the ways he writes.

OR

How does Priestley explore responsibility in An Inspector Calls? Write about:

the ideas about responsibility in An Inspector Calls

how Priestley presents these ideas by the ways he writes.

2017 Paper:

How far does Priestley present Mrs Birling as an unlikeable character? Write about:

what Mrs Birling says and does in the play

how Priestley presents her by the ways he writes.

OR

How does Priestley use the character of the Inspector to suggest ways that society could be improved?

Write about:

what society is shown to be like in the play and how it might be improved

how Priestley presents society through what the Inspector says and does.

Can you see the pattern? That's right - one character-based question and one theme-based question. That's pretty normal, so you can

. the same in your exam.

ju may be thinking 'aha, I feel lucky - if it was Sheila and Mrs Birling previously then it wont be them in my exam'. Think again. They may well choose the same character but ask you to focus on a different part of their personality. So make sure you revise every character.

What you'll also notice is that the question asks you to look both at **what the characters say** and **how Priestley presents them**. So that means focusing on **stage directions** as well as speech. This is really important: you'll be marked on your understanding of the play *as a play*, so you have to how how stage directions are used to add detail to the characters.

WHICH ONE TO TACKLE?

Now, I'll give you a little heads-up. Have a guess which of the questions most candidates go for? You've probably worked it out - most go for the character-based question as they think it will be easier. And in many ways it might be. But you want to get a grade 8 or 9, don't you? Of course you do. So don't immediately jump onto the character bandwagon as this might limit you.

The reason I'd suggest you looking at the theme-based question is that it can often allow you explore more complex ideas, bringing in all the characters and saying a lot about how Priestley uses them to present some big ideas about the world. Take the society improving question: you can say an awful lot there about class and prejudice and bring in some historical context to back up your points. Remember though that you're not writing a history essay: just a sentence or two about history, not paragraphs.

THE CHARACTER-BASED QUESTION

Let's have a think about how we'd go about answering this question:

How far does Priestley present Mrs Birling as an unlikeable character? Write about:

- what Mrs Birling says and does in the play

- how Priestley presents her by the ways he writes.

Here's a foolproof way of tackling this in the exam. You can use this approach for any character-based question.

- First of all, make sure you understand exactly what the question is asking of you. I'd always suggest **underlining the key words**, and making sure that every single thing you write in response refers in some way to those words. In this case it is about how Mrs Birling is **unlikeable**.
- Now, you're going to race to the pages in the play that focus on Mrs Birling. And pen in hand you'll go through everything she says and **underline anything** that shows us what an unpleasant woman she is. Think about how she speaks to her family as well as how she speaks to the Inspector. Look also at the **stage directions** - it's not just what she says, but also how she says it. This is important when writing about a play.
- I'd then suggest you jot down a **quick paragraph plan** so you know the order in which you'll write. Chronologically (order of events) is perfectly fine with character studies - in fact I'd usually suggest this as it makes it easier to show how a character might change (or not in the case of Mrs Birling):

- First impressions - stage directions and first things she says
- How she speaks to Sheila
- How she first responds to the Inspector
- How she acts when questioned
- How she acts once the Inspector has left

- 4-5 paragraphs is enough for an exam essay like this. Writing this short plan will help keep you focused, as everything you write in that paragraph will link to the subject of the paragraph and the key words in the question. Notice I don't include an introduction or conclusion? In an exam, with a limited amount of time, I would always suggest getting started on the analysis asap without spending time on a longwinded intro. One sentence max.

THE THEME-BASED QUESTION

Unsurprisingly, the approach to answering the theme-based question isn't much different to the character-based question. Let's look at this one:

How does Priestley explore responsibility in An Inspector Calls? Write about:

- the ideas about responsibility in An Inspector Calls

- how Priestley presents these ideas by the ways he writes.

- Start by underling the **key word or words** in the question. In this case it's **responsibility**.
- Locate the parts of the play where we see characters talking about responsibility. You'd expect to say a fair bit about the Inspector here, but think also about how the Birlings expect their children to act in a certain way - they have responsiblities as the Birlings children, however distorted these might be.
- Design your paragraph plan. However, rather than going through this chronologically, you can break the theme down into sub-themes, like this:

- Birling's responsibilities as an employer - how he differs in his thoughts on this compared to the Inspector and Eric

- Sheila's responsibility as a wealthy woman - how she abused this
- Gerald's and Eric's responsibilities as men - how they abused this
- Mrs Birling's responsibilities as a woman of importance and status
- The Inspector's concluding comments

You can probably see that by tackling the theme-based question like this, you have the possibility of saying an awful lot. Remember that theme is explored through characters and how they interact with one another, so it makes sense to look at how each of the characters develops this theme. It might not always work out like this, but if you can say something about each of the main characters this means you should have plenty to say.

You'll approach writing the essay in the same way as before. Punchy sentence to start the paragraph followed by PEAL. However, you might want to write a short introduction and conclusion for this sort of answer. Why might this differ? Because you may wish to put the theme in context at the beginning and sum up what Priestley is saying about the theme at the end. You'll say no more than 1-2 sentences for each, however - most of the marks will come in your main paragraphs.

Let's go into a bit more depth with how to construct a top grade paragraph.

HOW TO BUILD A PARAGRAPH

For those of you who've read my English Language book (do give it a go - I think it's quite useful), you'll know I have a certain way of structuring analysis. You'll probably have heard of PEE - Point, Evidence, Explanation - and that's ok. However, I prefer **PEAL - Point, Evidence, Analysis, Link**. Why? Because it's important that you show how your ideas develop throughout the paragraph. An examiner will be looking at this carefully. If you offer one quote and say one thing about it, you're looking at a 4 or 5. If you say 2-3 things, adding detail and **making links between quotes**, you'll be moving up to the 6,7 or more.

BEGIN BY MAKING YOUR POINT WITH A SHORT, PUNCHY PARAGRAPH OPENER

Begin every paragraph with a **short, punchy sentence** which shows the examiner exactly what you're going to be writing about in that paragraph. Here are a couple of examples:

- 'Both the opening stage directions and the first things Mrs Birling says give us a good indication as to the sort of woman she is.'
- 'When Mrs Birling speaks to Sheila we get the impression of a woman who is used to controlling her family and always has something to say.'

This is a great way to make it super easy for the exam marker to read your essay which will bring a smile to their face.

One thing to remember: you will only explore that particularly sentence opener in that paragraph. So if it's a paragraph about the opening stage directions, then this is the only thing you'll refer to. The tighter you can make your paragraphing the better your marks will be, as most students won't do that. But you're not most students, are you?

BRINGING IN YOUR EVIDENCE

Once you've set out exactly what you'll be exploring in the paragraph, it's time to bring in some quotes.

Let's use our first bullet point above as an example. You're going to bring in a few choice words and phrases, not great long chunks of text. It might be something like this:

Even before we are introduced to Mrs Birling we get a sense of the sort of woman she is by the home in which she lives.

After detailing the room in which the entire play is s
Priestley says that 'The general effect is substantial and
comfortable and old-fashioned but not cozy and homelike'.

What we've done there is introduce where the quote is, and then feed the quote into the sentence. You can see that the quote fits into the sentence without using punctuation. This is a better technique than continually stopping and starting a sentence with a colon for example.

MOVING INTO ANALYSIS

From here, it's where you'll be moving up into the 6s and above. Think of the opening sentences as being in the 4s and 5s grade-wise. It's only when you start to analyse that you start to get the good marks.

Your analysis section might look like this:

We get the impression of a woman with some wealth but perhaps not much concern about how others feel. By referring to the room as not being 'cozy' and 'homelike', Priestley suggests that Mrs Birling has no interest in creating a comfortable home for her family. It is more about appearances than anything more family-focused.

This is moving in the right direction, but to really nail this paragraph we need to bring in some **context**.

ADDING CONTEXTUAL DETAIL

Remember that you are writing a literature essay, not a language essay. And as such you have to make sure you include something on context.

In this case you'd be referring to why Mrs Birling is so unpleasant - much of this is because she is an upper class snob. So you'd be referring to the class system in 1912 England. Don't forget this.

A sentence might therefore look like this:

> A key theme of the play explores the notion of social class around the turn of the 20th century. For the Birlings, it is vital that others see their success, so how the room is furnished becomes important.

HOW TO GET TOP MARKS: WHAT TO LOOK FOR

We've seen one example of how to construct a paragraph. Let's look further at what the examiner is expecting to see in a top answer. This is taken directly from the mark scheme:

> At the top of the level, a candidate's response is likely to be a critical, exploratory, well-structured argument. It takes a conceptualised approach to the full task supported by a range of judicious references. There will be a fine- grained and insightful analysis of language and form and structure supported by judicious use of subject terminology. Convincing exploration of one or more ideas/perspectives/contextual factors/interpretations.

So what is this asking of you? Let's break it down.

- **A critical, exploratory and well-structured argument.** Get under the surface of the play. Don't settle for the easy or obvious answer. Inject your own point of view - don't just regurgitate York Notes (I've actually tried to give you some more original opinions throughout this revision guide so do use these as a starting point for your own ideas and responses). Explore different interpretations ('On the one hand.... On the other...). Quote, analyse, then analyse some more. Say a lot about a little, rather than a little about a lot.

- **A conceptualised approach.** This is an extension of the above: the top answers will explore big ideas, not be limited by simple character descriptions. Always have in the back of your mind the fact that characters are only there to allow the writer to explore these big themes and concepts. They are not real people.
- **Full range of judicious references.** This doesn't mean long quotes. You're going to be aiming for shorter quotes, taking them from different parts of the play, and including stage directions. If you start each paragraph with a clear indication as to what you're going to be exploring in that paragraph, and ensure every quote links to this, your quotes will be judicious (well-chosen).
- **A fine-grained and insightful analysis of language and form and structure**. Get into the small details. Look at individual words, always considering why Priestley chose one word over another. Remember those stage directions, and think about what they add to your understanding of character and theme. Remember that you're writing about a play - how does this fact impact your analysis? For example, if you don't have narrative description, how does the play give you a sense of time and place?
- **Judicious use of subject terminology.** Playwright not writer. Scenes not chapters. Lines not paragraphs. Stage directions not description. Get the idea? Use the language of drama, not novels or poems. Here are a few others you might like:
- Mise en scene - literally means 'put in the scene': it's the props, costume, lighting, staging - in fact everything outside of what the characters do and say.
- DL - downstage left - that's the area of the stage nearest the

audience, to the left as the characters look (so the audience's right)

- UR - upstage right - the area at the back of the stage, and on the right as the characters look (and so on)

- **Convincing exploration of one or more ideas/perspectives/contextual factors/interpretations.** This is what separates the grade 8 or 9 from the 7 and below. Originality. It;s honestly quite hard to teach this - some students just seem to have more ability to think in this original way than others. That's not to say that you can't give yourself a really good chance of getting the top grades by reading the play over and over, continually thinking about how each thing the character says tells us about them and the themes they explore. The more you prepare, the more original you're likely to be. Remember that vomiting up York or Letts won't get you these top grades? Why? Because everyone else will be doing that and the examiner will know these guides so will know if you're spewing up unoriginal stuff. Use them by all means, but don't rely on them. Same goes for this guide.

Ok, let's look at a couple of exemplar paragraphs that use these pointers and would get you a good mark.

THE CHARACTER-BASED ANSWER

If we use the indicators outlined in the previous section, we should be aiming to write paragraphs like this. Let's take the first one, which is all about **Mrs Birling being unlikeable**.

We can start by looking at the particular things the examiner will wish to focus on when marking this question. Again, this is taken from the mark scheme:

AO1

What Mrs Birling says and does

Sheila and Eric's reactions to her throughout

Her comments and reaction to the Inspector

Her lack of progression even after the revelations OR her refusal to back down in the face of the Inspector's questions

AO2

Presentation of her high-handedness when dealing with the Inspector and her children

Presentation of her snobbish approval of Gerald

Presentation of her reactions to the revelation about her Committee

The irony of her comments about the unborn child given that it would have been her own grandchild

AO3

Ideas about social class and her superior class to her husband

Ideas about non-acceptance of guilt/ blame

Her loyalty to her husband's view of the how the world works

Her alacrity in welcoming the news about the non-existence of the Inspector and her imagined despair when final phone-call is made

---

Here's the sample paragraph (not the whole essay, just a part to show the approach you should aim for with each paragraph):

From the very opening of the play, Mrs Birling is presented as an unlikeable matriarch who seeks to control her family and ensure they remain within the strictly defined parameters of upper class society. The opening stage directions very much set the scene: Priestley describes Mrs Birling as a 'cold woman and her husband's social superior'. She is cold because of her sense of social superiority, rather aloof because she sees herself as above the others in the room. It is also significant that she is Mr Birling's social superior. This immediately changes the power dynamic between the couple, compromising Birling's expected role as patriarch. Because class is not something you can leave, no matter how far Birling climbs up the career ladder, his wife will always be his superior. It is the anxiety that comes from this that drives much of Birling's actions.

Can you see what I did there? Began with a clear introduction to the paragraph, brought in quotes, and explored them. But also look at the language I use: matriarch, parameters, attributes. The grades 8 and 9 will have these sorts of words in abundance. Don't be shy to use more sophisticated language, providing you don't overdo it and mask what you're trying to say (in other words don't be clever just for the sake of it).

What I also aimed to do at the end of the paragraph is make a concluding remark - in this case about how Mrs Birling's superiority causes her husband's anxiety. This is also about the length of paragraph you should be aiming for - not so long that it's hard to follow, but also not a few sentences long. Take an idea, explore it, then explore it some more. Always be looking for that one more sentence that really gets into the detail.

We can carry on into the next paragraph with a new introductory sentence:

This haughtiness continues when she addresses the members of her family. She admonishes her husband for asking her to 'thank cook' for the meal. She says reproachfully 'you're not supposed to say such things', which indicates to us that the most important thing to Mrs Birling is how people act. There is a strict set of protocols within which she expects her family to operate, an etiquette which anyone who wishes to be part of her circle should follow. The fact that she is almost telling off her husband for something so seemingly innocuous is a clear indication of a woman who privileges these rules over any degree of warmth in her relationship with her family. To Mrs Birling, there can be nothing other than following predetermined expectations: always doing and saying the right thing. It is this approach to her family that presents her as unlikeable and unfeeling.

You can probably see here how much I say about one small quote. That is totally fine. You might actually spend an entire paragraph talking about one word: examiners love that, as it is showing how deeply you're getting into the text. You can also see the language I use: admonishes, etiquette, protocols. All of this adds up to an answer that's heading for a Grade 8 or 9.

THE THEME-BASED ANSWER

Here's the detail from the mark scheme for the question on responsibility - what the examiner is looking for:

AO1

Response to the characters with possible treatment of who is more aware of idea of social responsibility

Reactions to idea of the Inspector in terms of how he affects the characters as well as how he offers an opportunity to learn/change

Different characters' attitudes towards responsibility: Mrs Birling's hypocrisy, Mr Birling's treatment of his workers

Differences between older and younger generations' response to Inspector and Eva Smith

AO2

The use of the Inspector as dramatic device to enable characters to learn about responsibility

Any comments related to the presentation of character: Mr Birling's attitude towards others, contrast between Mr Birling and Eric/Mrs Birling and Sheila

Presentation of anger/bluster/defensiveness

Use and effects of pauses, hesitancy, dashes to suggest discomfort

AO3

Treatment of idea of responsibility as social issue

Comments dealing with wider ideas of class consciousness

Contrast between family's light-hearted relief and final shock of telephone call – used as punishment for self-satisfaction

Ideas about Eva Smith as metaphor

You'd be forgiven for thinking that this seems quite complex: there are some challenging ideas here. But this is the whole point about the theme-based question and why I'd usually recommend it for those of you who are aiming for the top grades. Because themes are, by their very nature, more complex than one character, you're able to say potentially more.

That's really not to say that you should avoid the character-based question. Not at all. If you feel you can explore these big themes and ideas through the character, then go for it. What I'm saying is that you have no choice but to explore these big ideas when you do the theme-based question. See how you feel in the exam.

Here's a sample paragraph:

When the Inspector arrives, Birling is lecturing Eric and Gerald over responsibility. As far as Birling is concerned, every man should look after himself. But, 'the way some of these cranks talk and write now, you'd think everybody has to look after everybody else, as if we were all mixed up like bees in a hive.' Birling disagrees with the idea that we have a responsibility towards others in the world: as long as we look after ourselves and our families nothing else matters. The 'cranks' he refers to are people like Priestley himself, writers, thinkers and politicians who want the world to take more responsibility for the welfare of those less fortunate than ourselves. At the time the play was set, laws were being passed to protect the rights of children, the old and unemployed. It would appear that Birling disagrees with this as it could lead to us losing our individuality and becomes like 'bees in a hive'. This is a good example of the contrast between capitalism and socialism: capitalists want to preserve their separation and individuality, whereas socialists want us to work more closely together.

You can probably see how I have tried to tick all the boxes here for a top grade. Quotes with detailed analysis - notice how I refer back to the longer quote twice when picking it apart. Something on context - who the 'cranks' are. And good, clear, accurate use of language.

This is another reason the theme-based question can enable you to get the higher marks - themes are products of the time texts are written or set: if you think about the sorts of themes around nowadays (such as #metoo) you'll see them in books and films in a way you might not have done ten or twenty years ago. So, when you dig into the theme you're more likely to be able to link it to the time the play was written.

5

HOW TO REVISE

Well done! You've got to the end of the play, made lots of notes, annotated your play text, and are ready to revise.

But wait: how do you do revise efficiently? There's a useful technique I'd like to share with you which I hope will help. Follow this plan to maximise your time.

1. REMIND YOURSELF OF THE AOS AND CHECK OUT THE MARK SCHEME

First of all, take the time to remind yourself of what you'll be examined on. Go back through the section on AOs from earlier in this book and list the key words. It might look something like this:

- AO1 - close reading of the play, small details, analysis, quotes
- AO2 - Language used, layout, fact it's a play so you need to write about it as a play with performers etc.
- AO3 - Social historical context - say something about the time it was written and set
- AO4 - Make sure answer is clearly laid out and focus on spelling and keeping handwriting legible.

Now, as you compile your notes, you can keep these in mind. The more you remember them the more likely you are to make sure everything you revise for falls into one of these buckets.

Look again at the sorts of things you'll be marked on with specific questions. For example, if we look back at the answer on Mrs Birling, we can see the areas the examiner wants to focus on:

- What Mrs Birling **says** and **does**
- Sheila and Eric's **reactions** to her throughout
- Her **comments and reaction** to the Inspector
- Her lack of progression even after the revelations OR her refusal to back down in the face of the Inspector's questions

AO2

- **Presentation** of her **high-handedness** when dealing with the Inspector and her children
- **Presentation** of her **snobbish approval** of Gerald
- **Presentation** of her **reactions** to the revelation about her Committee
- The **irony of her comments** about the unborn child given that it would have been her own grandchild

AO3

- Ideas about **social class** and her superior class to her husband
- Ideas about non-acceptance of **guilt/ blame**
- Her **loyalty** to her husband's view of the **how the world works**
- **Her alacrity** in welcoming the news about the non-existence of the Inspector and **her imagined despair** when final phone-call is made

It will be the same for each character and each exam question.

For the **character-based question**, **AO1** is about what characters say and do, how others react to them, and how characters progress through the play. **AO2** is about how the character is presented - the language used, stage directions etc. **AO3** is about how the writer explores ideas about the world through their writing.

For the **theme based question** it's quite similar.

- **AO1** will want you to explore how the characters respond to the themes of the play (such as how Birling deals with social class versus the Inspector, say). It will ask you to show how characters' actions and reactions illustrate the themes and what this says about them.
- **AO2** asks you to think about how characters are used as dramatic devices to explore the theme being examined (remember back to the opening of the chapter on characters). How their characters are presented, how their actions and reactions explore the theme, and how their emotions illustrate it. You should also remember here that you're writing about a play: so refer to stage directions, any pauses, nervous laughter etc. Not just what they say but also the directions the writer gives the actors.
- **AO3** is all about how the writer treats the theme, and what his wider comments are on it. What are they trying to show about the theme through their writing? Are there any characters that could be seen as metaphors (symbols) of the theme? The example here is Eva Smith seen as a symbol for how the working class were treated at the time.

The reason this is helpful to do before you start is that you can now structure your revision notes around these headings, so that when you write them up neatly and clearly you know which bucket they fall into. It's honestly a bit of a tick list but don't see that as limiting - it's actually quite liberating to work within a framework.

2. GRAB SOME A4 PRINTER PAPER AND COLOURED PENS

Next up you're going to grab a decent amount of printer paper (steal some from a parent's home office is my advice - just make sure you don't take it all they might need to print out a report later on). Or if you prefer, use loose leaf lined A4 paper. I prefer the freedom of not having lines but that's just me!

Take a piece, put the name of a character in bold at the top. Now, go back through your notes and as you do, pick out the **key words and phrases** that you've made a note of that describe the character.

So, for Birling it might be *patriarch, arrogant, selfish, self-important, anxious about status, bully, social climber*

Now, for each of those words you're going to find some **quotes**. Use each character word as a heading, and list quotes underneath. List each quote in one colour.

Then, in another colour, write a **short analysis** of what this quote tells you about this aspect of the character's personality. For example:

Patriarch: "if you don't come down sharply on these people, they'll soon be asking for the earth." - Sees himself as the father figure needing to control his workers like a parent.

Try to keep your analysis short and to the point - you're not writing an essay here, just enough to remind you **how the quote adds detail to the character trait**.

Now, in another colour, make any notes on what this quote is telling about **social and historical context**. In the example above you might write this:

Patriarch: "if you don't come down sharply on these people, they'll soon be asking for the earth." - Sees himself as the father figure needing to control his workers like a parent. Priestley suggesting here that capitalist progress meant that workers needed to be <u>controlled</u> like children in order to assure a business's success.

You may also wish to underline the most important words so they really burn into your memory.

This will form the bulk of your revision work on character. There are only so many character traits that you can pick out, and only so many quotes, so this won't take forever, providing you took the time to go through the play carefully making notes as you did. And if you've not done that yet, make sure you do that first. There can be no substitute for close and careful reading of the text.

Why colours? You don't have to, of course, but what you'll find is that, by using the same colours for quotes, analysis and context, you'll train your brain to always ensure you have all three colours as you compile your notes, and even when you're in the exam you'll be reminded of those colours and will ensure you cover all the AOs.

3. NOW, MOVE ON TO THEME

You're going to do the same thing now for the main themes of the play. Put one theme at the top of a new sheet of paper, find your quotes, write a short sentence about them, then add something about context. See character and theme revision as being the same when it comes to formatting your notes.

SHOULD I USE FLASH CARDS?

Flash/revision cards are really popular and can be helpful. The only problem I have with them is that they're quite small, and you can't fit much onto them. However, there are A5 versions which I think are more useful, and if you have small, neat handwriting then they might be a good bet. However, I think A4 paper is as good as anything as you can hole punch the sheets once you've written them up and put them into a folder which will keep everything neat.

I guess it's up to you which method you prefer!

6

THANKS FOR READING!

That's it for now! I hope this guide proved useful. If it did, please do leave me a review on Amazon. It would be much appreciated.

And do also check out my GCSE English Language revision guide, where I take you step by step through the AQA 9-1 Paper.

Best of luck when you enter that murky old world of the examiner's head! Don't be scared. They're human too.

Printed in Great Britain
by Amazon